Game Day

Game Day

50 Fun Spirit Fleece Projects to Sew

Cindy Cummins

with Allyce King and the
Creative Chicks of DIYStyle™
Photographs by Jack Deutsch

 St. Martin's Griffin
New York

GAME DAY. Text copyright © 2014 by Cindy Cummins. Photography copyright © 2014 by Jack Deutsch. Photographs on pages 6, 8, 9, 10, 11, 12, 13, 14, 15, 16 copyright © 2014 by Carmen Troesser. All rights reserved. Printed in the United States of America. For information, address St. Martin's Press, 175 Fifth Avenue, New York, N.Y. 10010.

www.stmartins.com

Design by Susan Walsh

The written instructions, photographs, designs, patterns, and projects in this volume are intended for personal use of the reader and may be reproduced for that purpose only.

The Library of Congress Cataloging-in-Publication Data is available upon request

ISBN 978-1-250-03097-9 (trade paperback)
ISBN 978-1-4668-5593-9 (e-book)

St. Martin's Griffin books may be purchased for educational, business, or promotional use. For information on bulk purchases, please contact Macmillan Corporate and Premium Sales Department at 1-800-221-7945, extension 5442, or write specialmarkets@macmillan.com.

First Edition: May 2014

10 9 8 7 6 5 4 3 2

For Mom and Dad

My real-life champions, game to take on just about

anything and everything . . .

you both encouraged me to Dream Big.

CONTENTS

INTRODUCTION

Sewing cute fashion has been a lifelong journey for me. Starting with the inevitable Barbie clothes, quickly working through making my first jumper in 4-H, whipping up gowns for the Homecoming Court, and on to stitching up an entire wardrobe of clothes through high school and college, sewing has always been a huge part of my life! Armed with a degree in clothing and textiles (and some divine intervention), I set out to make my mark in the sewing arena with serger sewing. As a result of this "new" sewing tool, and the hunger for new techniques, I designed the first serger pattern, *Coat in a Day,* and subsequently wrote numerous articles, as well as two books on the subject. Yes, I was a serger sewing fiend!

Fast forward to a few years later and add to the mix my fashionista and fashion designer daughter, Allyce King. After some trial video podcast webisodes, Allyce and I built the DIYStyle concept, brand, and Web site at *DIYStyle.net.* Reaching out to a fashion-minded DIY audience, our easy-to-follow instructions and trendy projects captured the attention of the sewing world. Led by a group of innovative women, and a growing entourage of associates and interns, we were dubbed the Creative Chicks! I ultimately became the "Mother Hen" to this twenty-something generation of creative craft and fashion designers, sewers, and bloggers, and our Web site grew quickly. Several video podcasts and projects later, and thanks to fashion reality television for the skyrocketing fashion DIY interest, we put quick-and-easy fashion sewing in the hands of stylish trendsetters everywhere.

Allyce's experience of designing for knit fabrics, coupled with my experience in the serger and knits sewing arena, plus a conversation with our editor, BJ Berti, put us on the track for creating a book of fabulous fun fleece projects and voila!: The book *Game Day—50 Fun Spirit Fleece Projects to Sew* was born! Wonderfully forgiving for a newbie sewer, as well as available in literally thousands of

prints, solids, and textures, fleece fabrics have taken over the fabric stores en masse. We have structured *Game Day* to provide a whole playbook of fun and stylish fleece projects, including items for the entire family (pets, too!), and designed them to be as fast and easy to create as possible. We know that you want to SEE the Big Game . . . not necessarily SEW your way through it! Few, if any, of these projects take more than an afternoon to make, and some can be completed in less than an hour. To help ease you along, included are useful tools, tips, and techniques to ensure that you create with success. And, to make sure that you have the lowdown on the most popular teams and their official colors, there are team charts and resources at the back of the book, so you can create with confidence.

What fun to make and show off *Game Day* gear, whipped up by you, in all of your favorite team colors and licensed team prints. Watching the Big Game will be done in YOUR style now!

Sew On Everyone!
Cindy Cummins
www.diystyle.net

FUN FLEECE

Fabulous fleece is the most forgiving and easy to sew fabric that can be found nearly everywhere that fabric is sold. We love this fabric for its warmth, easy care, and super-soft texture. You probably have a bunch of items in your home right now that are made from fleece fabric. Stitching up this synthetic fabric is *so* easy, and the myriad choices in solids, prints, textures, and varieties makes it simply fun to create projects that reflect your own personal style.

Originally, fleece was created as a recycled product fabric. Many manufacturers still use recycled water bottles as the main component of this fabric, but multiple varieties have evolved since Malden Mills brought this revolutionary fabric to the market more than thirty years ago. Fleece fabric was invented as a lighter weight and water repellant alternative to wool, with super-insulating properties attributed to the loft of the fabric and the air trapped between the brushed fibers. Different from traditional cotton and poly sweatshirt

fabrics with only one brushed side, fleece is soft and fuzzy on both sides—making this fabric cozy times two.

Most fleece (aka Polar Fleece) is 100 percent polyester, but some of the newer varieties have rayon or Lycra added to increase softness and drape, as well as stretch and recovery. No matter which type of fleece you choose for your project, you can be sure it will be a snap to sew, and any "wonky" stitching can usually be hidden in the depths of its loft. For that reason, it is one of the easiest fabrics for a beginner to work with, and all ages love its washable, easy care.

Know Your Fabric

FLEECE LOFT AND WEIGHT

Fleece comes in different thicknesses (or weights) that directly affect the types of projects for which it is best suited. The weight is measured by the amount of loft and thickness of the fabric. The thicker the fabric, the higher the number associated with its weight.

- 300 Weight Fleece weighs approximately 16 ounces per yard and is suitable for coats, vests, and heavy blankets.
- 200 Weight Fleece weighs approximately 12½ ounces per yard and is the most common weight of fleece found in fabric stores, and is available in solids, prints, and sculpted textures. It is ideal for the majority of your fleece projects including blankets, pillows, light jackets, hoodies, bottom-weight clothing such as pants and pajama bottoms, hats, scarves, and mittens.
- 100 Weight Fleece weighs approximately 9½ ounces per yard and is thinner than the heavier fleece weights, while still retaining the same desired insulation and waterproof properties. It is a good choice for any item where less loft is preferred, such as the lining in a coat or in a light pullover or sweatshirt.
- Microfleece weighs approximately 8 ounces per yard and is very thin, resembling a chamois cloth. It is a good choice for light and warm weight clothing items like a pullover tee, sleepwear, or leggings.

FLEECE FABRIC TYPES

- Anti-Pill. This fabric finish prevents the surface of fleece from balling or pilling up after wear and washing. Much preferred to cheaper fleece, this treatment will help increase the longevity and appearance of your fleece project.
- Cuddle. Super soft, this microfiber fleece is sometimes known as "Minky" and is wonderful for luscious baby blankets, throws, and robes. It tends to shed while you are sewing with it, but it is worth the sewing room mess in exchange for the extremely soft textured fabric that earns its name.
- Sculpted and Textured. This fleece fabric has the same 100% polyester base fabric as most 200 weight fleece, but with a textured or embossed surface. Some popular textures are rosettes, fur-look, ribs (that resemble corduroy), and dots.
- Fleece with Spandex. Add the stretch and recovery of spandex to fleece and you have a wonder fabric! This is the perfect fleece for headbands, leggings, and close-fitting tops. Athletes adore the warmth and movement that this fleece provides.

Know Your Teams!

Whether you are rooting for your local high school team, your college alma mater, or your favorite national football, baseball, basketball, or hockey team, you will want to get the colors right when making your *Game Day* gear. Of course, when you purchase a licensed imprinted fleece, you can be assured that the colors are spot on.

To make it easy for you when choosing the solid colors that represent your favorite team, we have included a number of useful charts at the back of this book to help you get it right. We list the top national teams in the NFL, MLB, NBA, and NHL. Also included are the top college teams in the NCAA. Refer to the charts, and make notes of your own for your local high school team so you can get sewing with the true colors of your chosen team!

Notions and Tools of the Trade

Here is a list of the basic and specialty tools you will want to have stashed in your sewing room for working with fleece. We have divided the list into two groupings: the Kit, which includes the basic tools and notions every seamstress needs to have to complete even the simplest of sewing tasks, and Specialty Notions and Handy Helpers. These are all of the extras you will need to make whipping up *Game Day* fleece projects quick and easy.

The Kit

Sewing Box. You will need a place to keep all of your tools so they are handy and convenient to move around. We absolutely love repurposing vintage train cases into sewing kits! Find a case in your local thrift shop and decorate the exterior to reflect your own personality and style. A low-cost alternative is a tackle box from the sporting goods store. It has plenty of

small sections for little parts and pieces. If you decide to go the tote-bag route for your supplies, make sure it has a bunch of pockets and a stiff bottom so it does not collapse when you set it on a surface.

12-inch Ruler. Measure twice cut once. Sewing has a lot to do with getting the right measurement, before you actually put fabric to a sewing machine. A clear ruler marked in $\frac{1}{8}$-inch increments that is 1 inch wide is our favorite for marking lines and creating patterns.

Seam Gauge. This handy 6-inch measuring gauge is probably the most used tool in our sewing box. Purchase a couple of these so you always have one ready to grab. The seam gauge has a sliding tab to set at the desired measurement, and has $\frac{1}{8}$-inch markings.

Tape Measure. The type of tape measure that you will need most often for

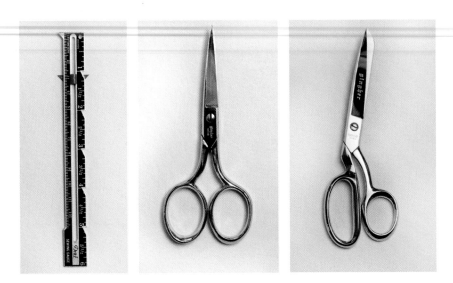

sewing is the flexible kind, not the metal kind that you get at the hardware store. Tape measures come in varying lengths, but a 60-inch long one will be just fine. Usually one side is marked in inches with ⅛-inch or smaller increments, and the flip side is marked in centimeters, with millimeter increments. We like the kind that rolls into its own case, making it easy to stash in your sewing kit or purse when needed.

Small, Sharp, Pointed Scissors.

A pair of small embroidery scissors that are sharp right to the tip is the key to getting slits, buttonholes, and intricate areas trimmed neatly. It's also handy to keep these beside the sewing machine so you get into the habit of trimming away those pesky thread ends as you are sewing.

Shears.
Do not confuse scissors with shears! Shears are bent along the lower edge to accommodate cutting on a flat surface. A pair of good 8-inch bent dressmaker shears are worth their weight in gold when you are cutting and sewing all types of fabric. There is nothing more frustrating than trying to cut through fabric with shears that are gnawing the fabric instead of cutting through it smoothly. My favorite brand is Gingher, and it has outlasted several others. We recommend stashing your shears in a safe place to ensure they do not end up in the wrong hands cutting things other than fabric because they were the sharpest "scissors" in the house!

Paper Scissors.
We keep several pairs of paper scissors handy, buying the inexpensive ones two and three at a time. Mark them "PAPER" with a permanent marker, and use them for all of the tasks that you don't want your fabric shears subjected to, such as cutting paper, fine wires, plastic, etc. Have some of these paper scissors out in

heads will not melt like the cheaper plastic-head pins will.

Magnetic Pincushion. Keeping all of your straight pins in order so that you can grab them quickly, and not spill them all over the floor of your sewing room, was a pain until these convenient magnetic pincushions surfaced. Plus, they are easy to swipe across an area to pick up any stray pins that may escape as you are working.

plain sight for those folks who tend to run off with your things, and it will help to keep your good shears safe and sound.

Buttonhole Cutting Kit. An extremely useful little tool set, a buttonhole cutter resembles a chisel with a super sharp straight edge blade attached to a handle. The cutter comes with a small mat or wooden block, so that you can cut a buttonhole or slit with a protective surface underneath.

Extra-fine Straight Pins. As you sew, you will be using a bunch of straight pins to hold pieces of a project together until you stitch it together with your sewing machine or serger. Glass head pins with at least a 1⅜-inch length, and a fine .50mm shaft are just the thing to help keep fleece and other fabrics tame and in place. A glass head is much better than plastic if any ironing is to take place, because the

Safety Pins. Pins that latch can be very helpful when trying to keep layers of fabrics from shifting or when you are fitting clothing, especially with kids. Buying an assortment pack with lots of sizes will ensure you have some of the larger ones that can be used to thread cords and elastics through casings, too.

Marking Tools. Transferring necessary marks onto fabric can be done in a multitude of ways. Since marking depends on the fabric and what is appropriate, it's great to stock up on a variety of these. Our kit includes a white chalk pencil, a water-soluble marking pen, an air-soluble marking pen, and several colors of chalk liners. The chalk liners are really handy and can mark a fine line that can be later brushed away. And the bonus is they are refillable.

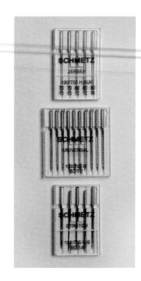

Hand Sewing Needles. There are many instances where you will need to stitch something by hand rather than by machine, so you will need an assortment of hand sewing needles in addition to the kind your machine takes. Choose an applique/sharps needle pack to start, then add in other sizes and types as you see fit. There are multipacks to choose from with an assortment of needle types and sizes; just be sure to purchase one that is high quality or the needles will not be smooth enough to glide easily through the fabric. One of our favorite needle brands has a Teflonlike coating to help the needle go through fabric like butter!

Beeswax. This is a hand sewer's best friend. Purchased as a small disk or block, beeswax will minimize the twisting and knotting of your thread. After threading your needle, and before you place a knot in the end, run the thread through the beeswax to coat. Knot your thread and stitch away.

Machine Sewing Needles. A sewing machine requires a needle to stitch, and you will need to keep several on hand to keep everything flowing in good working order. Sewing machine needles come in various sizes: 11, 12, 14, and 16 are typical U.S. sizes, while 70, 75, 80, and 90 are the European counterparts. They also come in different types, for the various fabric types we sew with. A universal sewing machine needle is used most widely, with specialty types like stretch, jersey, jeans, microtex, and embroidery being saved for specific stitching needs. There are even machine needles for sewing leather! Our favorite brand is Schmetz, and they have a huge array of sewing machine needle sizes and types. Here is a big sewing rule to remember: Change your needle after every project, even if it has not broken or caused

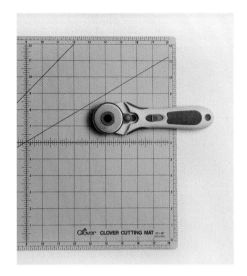

an issue. Sewing machine needles are really inexpensive, and are the number-one cause of skipped or unbalanced stitching. When in doubt, throw it out!

Pencil, Pen, and Notepad. We always keep a small notebook, pencil, and pen in our sewing kit. A little bound notebook is a great place to keep notes and measurements so you can refer back to past projects and generally keep organized.

Specialty Notions and Handy Helpers

Rotary Cutter and Cutting Mat. A rotary cutter and mat is to cutting what a microwave is to a kitchen (I say that about a serger, too!). Once you have added the tools into your basic kit, this is the one to add just after acquiring your good shears and sharp-tip scissors. A rotary cutter is a razor blade on a wheel and looks a bit like a pizza cutter. Rotary cutters come in small 28mm, medium 45mm, and large 60mm blade sizes. If you can only get one, choose the 45mm size. As you choose thicker fleece fabrics to cut through, the 60mm size is great for that, and the 28mm size is perfect for when you need to do more intricate cutting on curves. Be sure to choose a rotary cutter that is easy to open and close, as you will need to get into the habit of closing the cover after every cut for safety purposes.

You will also need the proper surface for the rotary cutter to cut on: a self-healing cutting mat (the larger the better in most cases). We use two mats of 24-inches × 36-inches, side by side, to cover a larger area. Mats are usually marked in 1-inch grids, making sizing up pattern pieces quick and easy. With see-through pattern paper and a gridded mat, enlarging a gridded pattern piece is a snap. There are many size mats to choose from; just

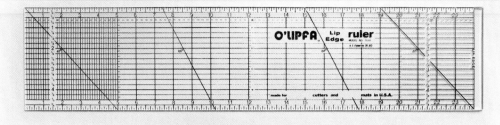

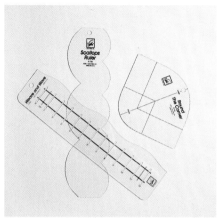

purchase the largest size you can afford and add other sized mats as your sewing evolves, as well as your budget!

Rotary Cutting Blades. Just like your sewing machine needs needles sharp and switched out regularly, you will want to do the same with the blades of your rotary cutter. Keep at least one backup blade that fits your cutter, and change the blade as soon as you notice any dullness or skipped cutting areas. In addition, there are "fancy" blades that fit most rotary cutters, including a wave blade and a pinking blade. Check the size of the blade and type to be sure that it is a fit for your handle. These are fun to keep on hand to "fussy

cut" edges and fabrics.

For example, we used a wave blade to create the fleece edging on the Tailgate Table Topper Throw, creating a quick self-fabric trim with a wavy scalloped raw edge.

Gridded Ruler. Rotary cutters are easy to control when used with a ruler as a guide. The clear acrylic rulers are best, as you can see the fabric through the ruler and follow the gridded markings to get straight cuts. We use one that has a "lip" on one end of a 5-inch × 24-inch ruler that helps it act as a T-square. This works wonderfully with a gridded mat, as you can lay fabric out and cut using both the guides on the ruler and the mat to get perfectly sized pieces.

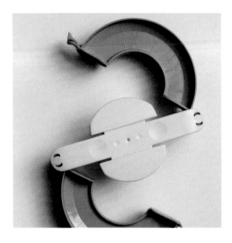

fabric to size, stitch in and out of the designated holes, snap off the template, and then pull thread to gather and knot. Voilà! Perfect yo-yos every time! Our favorite yo-yo templates are from Clover-USA and are available in many sizes and shapes. They work well with fleece fabrics, as well as with the quilt cottons they were originally designed for!

Acrylic Cutting Templates. There are several templates available that can be used as cutting guides for fabric. Made from clear acrylic, many of these templates also double as rulers, thanks to measuring guides printed on the template. One of our must-haves is a fringe-cut ruler/template. This handy, mat-style ruler has slots for your rotary cutting blade and will help you make perfectly aligned cuts—just right for neatly cut fringe on fleece. It also works great to cut multiple strips from a folded piece of fabric. You can purchase acrylic templates for flowers, rosettes, scallops, shapes, and more.

Yo-Yo Maker Templates. Making a yo-yo is a fun and easy embellishment that everyone, including the kids, can learn to create. However, it's not always easy to make several of the same size and with evenly spaced stitching for the gathers. With a yo-yo template, you merely snap your fabric between the plastic pieces, trim

Pom-Pom Maker. If you have ever tried to make a pom-pom with a piece of cardboard and yarn, you know how much of a challenge it can be. With this method, it is certainly not an exact process, and trying to keep all the cut pieces in place while you are tying the pom-pom is almost impossible. A pom-pom maker comes to the rescue. With swing-out arms to wrap on to, the maker not only measures automatically and holds the cut pieces securely while you tie it tight, but it also enables you to create a really full and fluffy pop-pom. We cut narrow ½-inch strips from fleece to make matching pom-poms for many of our projects in this book. Choose from several sizes of pom-pom makers; we used the small size for many of our trims on clothing and hats.

Wash-Away Basting Tape. Basting tape for sewing that washes away? That is exactly what this double-sided sticky tape is designed to do! It is absolutely

indispens-able for holding hook-and-loop closures, ribbons and trims, and even zippers in place without pins until you can stitch to secure. And the best part is you don't have to remove it! It will dissolve in the wash, leaving no trace of your hands-free helper.

Fabric and Gem Glue. You will need a fabric glue any time you are securing a fabric to another surface with adhesive. Glue made specifically for fabric dries inconspicuously (no bleed-through) and is widely available at any craft or sewing retailer. Similarly, when gluing gems onto fabric, a glue specifically formulated for gems is preferred. When gem glue dries, it is crystal clear and strong enough to keep the gem from falling off. We like to keep a supply of different types of sewing, craft, and gem glues on hand at all times.

Lint Roller. You may already have one of these tape-style lint removers in your linen closet. Break it out—you will need to have it handy when sewing with fleece to nab all of the stray bits of fuzz and scrap that seems to stick to your project, and YOU! In addition to the handy lint roller, you will want your household vacuum nearby to keep fleece bits from infiltrating unwanted places in your home.

Threads, Trims, and Closures

The components you select for your projects are just as important as the fabrics you use. Choose these necessary parts and pieces with care, and create with confidence.

All-Purpose Sewing Thread. Choose a high-quality thread to sew with both by hand and by machine. A 100 percent polyester thread is best for most of your sewing projects. Our thread of choice

is Dual Duty XP from Coats and Clark. A good-quality standard sewing thread comes in a large array of colors to match anything that you are sewing, and on a spool that minimizes the thread getting tangled on your sewing machine. Don't go for the cheap thread! If it is only available in a few colors and is in the bargain bin, leave it in the store and opt for a high-quality thread instead.

Serger Cone Thread. Instead of being sold on a spool, thread for a serger is put up on a cone, and with much more yardage than on the standard spool of thread. As with choosing a standard sewing thread, purchase quality, long-staple polyester cone thread. We have lots of A&E Maxilock thread in colors to match our projects. It is a good, low-lint, high-quality thread created especially for serger sewing. If you are new to serging, start collecting cones of the colors you sew most often—they will last quite awhile, stitching through lots of

projects. If you are in a pinch and finding yourself short of coordinating cone thread, place your best matching thread colors through the serger needle(s), as this is what may show in the serged seam of an item, and thread a neutral color through the loopers.

Hook-and-Loop Closure. You can use several different kinds of closures for fleece, but hook-and-loop closure is great, low profile, and easy for all ages to work with. Known to most of us as Velcro, this is the hook-and-loop fastener's trade-marked brand name, just as Kleenex is to facial tissue. For garment sewing, be sure to choose the sew-thru type, as your needle will get gummed up with the sticky-back types. One side, the rougher side, is the hook and the other, the softer side, is the loop. Placed together, the hooks nestle into the loops and create a secure closure. Pinning into hook-and-loop pieces can be tricky, so use wash-away basting tape to

hold them securely in place until stitching. Use a sharp needle and sew along the edges of the hook-and-loop tape, or between the rows, for easy sewing.

Elastics. There are probably more elastic varieties available than we can count. To edit this down a bit, there are really only a couple of types we use for the projects in this book: braided and nonroll. For a pull-on waist, choose a nonroll or braided ⅜-inch elastic (this fits all of the casings in the *Game Day* projects). For a stretchy drawstring, a ⅛-inch oval braided elastic fits into the cord locks perfectly. On a couple of projects, we used wide braided elastic as a component (see Flower Power Headwrap). Most elastic is sold in packages or by the yard in standard black and white, but colors are starting to crop up, too.

Fold-Over Elastic. We love this elastic edging! It has a channel in the center to enable the elastic to fold in half and serve as a binding. It is stretchy, so it gives with knit fabrics such as fleece and it finishes off an edge nicely. It used to be available only in standard black and white colors for the home sewer, but many more colors and widths are surfacing for sale at your local fabric retailer. We prefer the ⅝ inch to ¾ inch for clothing, and the wider 1 inch fold-over elastic for items such as bibs and blankets. Whatever your preference on width, once you start sewing with fold-over elastic, you will be hooked on how easy it is to apply and the professional durable finish that it provides.

Lycra Fabric as Edging. Since we love the look and durability of a stretchy binding on knits and fleece, but can't always find the color in the fold-over elastic we need, we started collecting Lycra swim fabric for use as an elastic binding. It is available in a wide range of solid colors and prints, and can be cut into strips with a rotary cutter to use as binding. We use a mock French binding sewing technique to achieve a nice neat look that resembles fold-over elastic. Check out the technique in the Strategy Book—Tips and Techniques chapter.

Sewing Machines and Sergers

Sewing Machines. Even the most basic sewing machine can sew fleece and knit fabrics. While a serger is a great addition to your sewing room (see next section), as long as your sewing machine is in good working order, and it can create the following stitches, you will have it made: straight, zigzag, and multistep zigzag. Yep, that's all you need! And most sewing machines have these three stitches included.

Of course, you will find certain features super convenient on a sewing machine. An automatic needle threader, thread cutter, needle up/down button, lock stitch (stitches in place to replace backstitching), and a computerized machine can make things go a little faster. If you are looking for a new machine, many of these features are standard on even the lowest-priced sewing machines. We always recommend shopping around and purchasing a sewing machine from an independent retailer in your local area who can answer questions about the machine and give you lessons or assist in any repairs.

Sergers. Hands down, we LOVE sergers! This nifty machine can trim, oversew an edge, and stitch the seam—all in one step. And it is a seam that is strong and yet gives with the fabric, especially suited to knit fabrics and fleece. A serger is a fantastic time-saver—think of a serger to your sewing room as a microwave is to your kitchen. Both of these reduce time spent in both of their respective areas, but do not replace the basic equipment. You will always want your sewing machine as the main creation station!

Sergers come in low-end to high-end models, depending on the bells and whistles included. One of the areas that can make all the difference on the serger you choose is the ease (or not) of threading. Since this machine requires four spools, instead of the one used by your sewing machine, it can be just a bit more intimidating. But it does not need to be! Check out several models at your local independent retailer before choosing one, so you know the ropes. Our favorite is a 2/3/4 thread serger that can create a lot of stitch variations, and is still a snap to rethread when needed.

If you already have a serger as part of your sewing room, a cover stitch is another machine that we use quite often. This machine makes a double or triple needle stitch on top of the fabric and an overlock finish on the underside, just like you see on many of your ready-to-wear garments. Although not a necessity, a serger and/or a cover stitch machine certainly makes for a well-outfitted sewing room capable of whipping up just about anything with ease and a professional look.

STRATEGY BOOK

Tips and Techniques

Fabric Prep and Cutting

Fleece fabrics do not need to be prewashed and require little, if any, preparation before cutting. There is a right side and a wrong side to fleece, even though some of the fabrics look virtually the same on both sides. On solids, the side that looks similar to needle-punched felt is the wrong side, and the non-pill, pebble-textured side is the right side of the fabric. With most prints, it is fairly obvious which side is the right side, especially if it has lettering or a directional print. The side that has the clearest image is considered the right side of the fabric. If you are still unsure, pull on a cut edge of the fleece and it will roll to the right side.

As with any fabric, fleece should be cut with right sides together or with the wrong side faceup and the right side facedown. Use long, fine, straight pins to secure patterns to the fabric. Choose a good pair of shears to cut fleece, and be aware that there will be some fuzz or lint debris as you cut out your pieces. Keep your vacuum handy!

Sewing and Serger Setup

SEWING

The key to getting good sewing results with fleece is to begin by using the correct stitch for each fleece application. Start each project with a new needle, either a universal size 12/80 or a stretch size 75/11 needle. These needles are good for most midweight to lightweight fleece. If you are sewing with a heavier fleece, choose a stronger universal or stretch needle. The following three stitches are used to create all of the projects in this book:

Straight Stitch. Use a 3.0 stitch length with matching high-quality thread in the needle and bobbin. This stitch is used most when sewing fleece on hems, topstitching, and securing edges.

Zigzag Stitch. The zigzag stitch is usually set at 3.0 stitch length and 1.0 stitch width. This setting gives the seaming property of a straight stitch but with some of the flex and give of the zigzag. Use this stitch for the majority of the fleece seams.

Multistep Zigzag Stitch. Use this sewing machine stitch when you need a stitch with a major amount of give. To create super flexible seams, set the machine at 3.0 stitch width and 2.0 stitch length. When applying a binding or fold-over elastic on an edge that needs to be able to stretch and recover, set the machine at 5.0 stitch width and 2.0 length (the wider stitch width will help secure the binding while leaving the elastic to bounce back after stretching).

SERGER SETUP

Choose the 3-thread- or 4-thread-wide serger overlock stitch for working seams or finishing the edges of fleece. Be sure to choose high quality cone thread for best results. A serged seam is nicely trimmed and neatly stitched, and gives with the fabric when necessary. Another advantage of using a serger instead of your sewing machine for seaming is the differential feed feature on most sergers. If your fleece is stretching out as you stitch, this feature can assist in easing the fabric layers together, achieving perfect results. Since fleece is a knit fabric with a fair amount of stretch, using a serger for a large portion of

the seaming of your projects is a natural.

As with your sewing machine, change the needles in your serger on a regular basis. This will help to cut down on skipped stitches and to prevent snags in your fleece. Watch your knife blades on the serger as well if you are doing a lot of fleece sewing. Fleece can dull the blades after a time, and they may need to be replaced along with the needles. This is inexpensive maintenance and can be done easily with a screwdriver and by following the directions in your serger guidebook.

Edges, Hems, and Finishes

RAW EDGE FINISH

Fleece is a fabric that does not ravel much, if at all, so it is fine to leave raw edges unfinished. You can also trim edges to shape with a wave or pinking rotary cutting blade. This opens up the possibilities of using fleece as a trim, by cutting strips and finishing edges with a fancy finish. Rotary cutting blades are handy and can be used with a straight-edge ruler to trim out strips of fleece in a jiffy. You can also trim logos and motifs from fleece, and stitch them back onto projects, leaving the motif edges unfinished.

FOLD-OVER ELASTIC BINDING

This stretchy binding is so easy to work with and it molds to curves just as easily as to straight edges. Increasingly, we are finding it in more colors beyond the standard white and black, making it a go-to edging when you want a professional finish on fleece. We have worked with this binding extensively and have learned a few tricks along the way that deliver great results. With this easy application tip you will learn to love this edging too! Try this superfast DIYStyle technique:

1. Apply the fold-over elastic to the wrong side of your project, placing the trim under the raw edge and matching the center fold on the elastic. Your project should have the right side of the fabric facing up, and the wrong side of the fold-over elastic facing up, as you get ready to sew. Using a narrow zigzag stitch, 1.0 wide and 3.0 long, stitch ¼" from the raw edge through all layers, catching the edge of the fold-over elastic.

2. Fold the elastic binding along the center fold line to the right side of your project. With a straight stitch, secure the edge of the binding, stitching close to the finished edge. Stretch the binding just slightly as you stitch to prevent broken stitches. For maximum stretch (where the fabric and the binding both will need a large amount of stretch and recovery), use a zigzag or multistep zigzag to secure this edge of the fold-over elastic.

MOCK FRENCH BINDING

Sometimes there is a color that really stumps us, making it a challenge for us to find a binding to match. So to increase our options, we use a "create-your-own" technique using Lycra spandex swimwear fabric. Cut this stretchy fabric into strips and fold over edges to form a binding. Now there are tons more match-up possibilities! Create the binding using this superfast DIYStyle technique:

1. Cut 2" strips the width of the Lycra spandex swimwear fabric for the greatest amount of stretch.

2. Place fabric strip along raw edge of fleece, right sides together. Stitch ¼" from edge. On long edges, pull strip slightly as you stitch to prevent the fleece edge from stretching out.

3. Fold the strip over the raw edge, snug to the wrong side, forming binding. Pin binding in place at intervals on the right side of project to hold. Stitch in the ditch (where the binding meets the fleece fabric) through all layers to secure.

4. Trim away excess spandex fabric on the wrong side of project, approximately ⅛" from stitching.

EASY DRAWSTRING CASING

There are so many times that we need an opening in a casing for a drawstring, but we don't want to go to the trouble of making buttonholes. With the easy drawstring method, all you need is the straight stitch on your sewing machine. All of the casings that have a cord or drawstring in this book use this superfast DIYStyle technique:

1. Pin the front seam with right sides together. Stitch the seam for 1", leave a 1" unstitched space to create the opening for the drawstring, then continue stitching the remainder of the seam. Be sure to lockstitch or backstitch to secure stitches.

2. Finger press the seam open. Stitch the opened seam allowance close to the seam line on both sides of the seam. Start at the upper waist edge and stitch down 2", securing the opened seam allowances to the project. This will keep the seam allowance from folding over when the elastic is inserted.

3. Fold over 1" to the inside edge to form the casing. Stitch close to the raw edge to secure.

4. Measure and cut a length of elastic to fit the waist (less 4 inches for babies and kids and 6 inches for adults). Cut two ties for the drawstring. Stitch a tie to each end of the length of elastic. Using a safety pin, thread the elastic drawstring tie through the casing. Adjust the elastic so the fullness is evenly distributed. Tie the drawstring ends into a bow or a knot.

Fleece Embellishments

Making decorative doodads from fleece is really easy. A few of our favorites are featured here and utilize some of the helpful gadgets.

Rosettes and Flowers. Gathered up tight, it's a rosette. Flatten it out a bit and you have a darling flower. No matter how you make these, be sure to glam them up with small buttons, rhinestones, and beads using this superfast DIYStyle technique:

1. Cut a strip of fleece 1½" to 2" wide × 30" long.

2. Round the ends of the long strip. Using a running stitch, gather the strip by hand spacing stitches ¼" apart. Gather the strip tight to 6 inches; knot threads to secure.

For Rosettes: Roll up the gathered strip with the raw gathered edge forming the bottom of "rose." Pin to hold through the layers. Stab stitch through the bottom layers several times, crossing stitches across the bottom of flower. Knot threads.

For Flowers: Swirl the gathered strip, overlapping the raw gathered edge until a flower is formed. Adjust until you have a nice flower shape. Stab stitch through the layers to hold. Stitch again around the center, pulling stitches tight to gather. Knot threads.

Yo-Yos. Little disks of gathered fabric… this technique is ages old! Today we can pop these babies out by the drove using an innovative, template style yo-yo maker. Our go-to gadget for these is from Clover-USA and comes in many shapes and sizes. You can even make clover shaped yo-yos! The largest templates work best with fleece, but you can use all of them with the thinner micro fleece fabrics using the following technique:

1. Cut a piece of fleece 1" larger all around than the yo-yo maker template.

2. Layer the fleece between the two yo-yo maker pieces. Make sure the fleece lies flat and smooth. Leave ½" of fleece around the template; trim away excess.

3. With buttonhole twist thread (or other strong thread) threaded through a hand needle, follow the markings on the template and stitch in and out of the yo-yo maker's holes. Stitch around the template through the layers until you are back to where you started.

4. Leaving the thread through the needle, carefully pop off the yo-yo maker.

5. Firmly draw up the thread to gather the yo-yo. You will need to pull tight on the threads to get a nice, evenly gathered yo-yo.

6. Keeping the yo-yo gathered tight, knot the thread on the inside of the yo-yo. Secure ends.

7. Repeat steps 1–6 and make a whole batch of these lovelies!

Optional: Stitch or glue a button, bead, or other finding in the center of the yo-yo if desired.

Pom-Poms. Making pom-poms used to mean cutting a piece of cardboard, wrapping it with yarn, and holding your breath while you cut the yarn ends. Then saying a few more choice words as the little yarn pieces fell out before you could get it tied up. You can still go that route, but we adore the pom-pom maker from

Clover Needlecraft. (Yes, there is a trend here with Clover-USA and ingenious sewing and craft gadgets!) It is pure genius how the arms on this thingy hold on to the pieces until it is tied and the maker removed. We use fleece strips in lieu of the yarn, and all of the sizes work well, small through extra-large, to make perfect fleece pom-poms every time. Use our superfast technique:

1. Open the arms on the pom-pom maker. Using ¼"–½" strips cut from fleece fabric, wind the strip around each set of arms, clipping the end of the fleece strip in between the arms to hold.

2. After winding each set of arms, fold the arms into the center. (We used two 60"-long strips on each set of arms for a full pom-pom. Use one 60" strip on each set for a looser pom-pom.)

3. Cut the fleece "yarn" through the center groove all around the pom-pom maker through all of the fleece strip layers.

4. Using a 9" long strip of fleece, tie the pom-pom tight with a double knot.

5. Open up each of the arms away from the pom-pom. Remove the maker and fluff.

6. Trim fleece ends as necessary to shape into a nicely rounded pom-pom. (Do not cut away the tie ends. You will need these to attach the pom-pom to your project!)

T-Shirt and Fleece "Surgery."

Many moons ago we started cutting pieces from T-shirts to sew back onto other projects as appliques. Both T-shirt fabric and fleece are similar with low- to no-ravel properties, so why not do the same with fleece? Any motif, team logo, or other graphic can be carefully cut ("surgery") from the fabric for use as an applique. We trim motifs so that we have about ½" or more of excess fabric from the outline where we will be stitching. We often cut rather wonky shapes, pin them onto our project where desired, and stitch following the outline of the logo or motif. It's easy when you have just a bit of extra fabric all around the desired finished shape to help stitch it on smoothly. You can always trim the extra off, but you certainly can't add it back on! Here is our technique:

1. Trim the desired motif from team-print fleece or a T-shirt. Leave at least ½" or more around the motif border from where you will be stitching.

2. Pin motif in place on the project. Use several straight pins to help prevent shifting.

3. Using a 3.0 length straight stitch, secure the motif on the project, stitching along the motif outline. Take care to stitch slowly and neatly. Use a lockstitch to secure threads at the start and end of stitching.

4. Trim away excess fleece or T-shirt fabric ⅛" away from stitching.

One

Winter Warm-Up

TIE ONE ON—SCARF ROUNDUP

Scarves are so quick to create with just a small amount of fabric. This is a perfect intro project if you have not yet had the opportunity to sew with fleece. Each of the first three styles uses straight lines of stitching—even a newbie sewer will be able to whip these up in time for kickoff. And for super-fast fashion, the Ruffled Loop endless scarf can be serged together in less than 20 minutes!

Pull Thru

SUPPLIES

¼ yard each, 2 solid-colors of fleece or team-print fleece

All-purpose sewing thread

CUT

Cut 2, 8" × 40" pieces of solid-color or team-print fleece

SEW

1. Place both fleece rectangles right sides together. Stitch around all outer edges, using a ½" seam allowance. Leave a 4" opening along the center of one long side.
2. Trim corners then turn scarf right side out. Hand stitch opening closed.
3. Find center of scarf by folding in half lengthwise. Mark this with a pin near one of the ends.
4. From the center-marked end of the scarf, measure 7" up from the finished edge and place a mark along the center. Measure and mark a 3" line from this point along the center to create a slit for the scarf to pull thru. Pin to hold both layers in place at both ends of this mark.
5. Using a straight stitch, stitch ⅛" away from the line all around, forming a narrow box. Use a sharp pair of scissors to cut the slit open. Pull finished scarf end through the slit opening.

Endless Loop

SUPPLIES

⅜ yard each, 2 coordinating
    solid-color fleece
⅜ yard, team-print fleece
All-purpose sewing thread

CUT

Cut 1, 10" × 18" piece from each of the solid colors of fleece
Cut 2, 10" × 18" pieces from the team-print fleece

SEW

1. Matching the short ends, place the right sides together, alternating the solid-color pieces with the team-print pieces. You should have print/solid/print/solid. Stitch seams.
2. Fold the long strip in half lengthwise, right sides together. Stitch the long seam, starting 3" from the end, and stopping 3" from the opposite end. Turn tube right side out.
3. Match the raw ends, right sides together, forming a loop. Stitch seam.
4. Slip stitch opening closed.

Ruched Scarf

SUPPLIES

¼ yard, solid-color fleece

¼ yard, coordinating
team-print fleece

2 yards, ⅜" elastic

1 yard each, ⅜" grosgrain ribbon
in 2 coordinating colors

All-purpose sewing thread

CUT

Cut 1, 6" × 60" piece from solid-color fleece.

Cut 1, 6" × 60" piece from team-print fleece.

SEW

1. Layer the fleece strips, raw edges matching, with wrong sides together. Mark the center lengthwise, then stitch through both layers to secure, from one end to the other. Take care to backstitch at each end.
2. Stitch a channel, ⅝" away from center stitched line, one on each side of the center line, creating two channels for the elastic.
3. Cut 2 pieces, 36" long, from the elastic. Cut 4 pieces, 18" long, from coordinating ribbon. Stitch each of the ribbon pieces to each end of the two elastic pieces.
4. Thread elastic into channels, with the ribbon ends left free at the ends of the scarf. Pull elastic to evenly distribute fullness to create the ruffles.

Ruffled Loop

SUPPLIES

⅓ yard each, 2 coordinating solid-color fleece

All-purpose sewing thread

CUT

Cut 4, 5" × 20" pieces from each, 2 coordinating solid-color fleece

SEW

Note: For these seams use either the rolled edge stitch on your serger, trimming away very little as you stitch, or a narrow 1.0 wide, 2.0 length zigzag stitch over the raw edge of the fleece to achieve the lettuce edge finish for this instant scarf.

1. Matching the short ends, wrong sides together, alternate colors of the solid-color pieces—2 of each color per strip, creating two long pieced strips. You should have solid 1/solid 2/solid 1/solid 2 for one strip and solid 2/solid 1/solid 2/solid 1 for the second strip. Stitch seams, stretching the seams as you sew, to get the ruffled effect.
2. Taking care to match the seamed intersections, stitch both long strips together, wrong sides together. Continue to stretch this seam as you sew for the same ruffle effect.
3. Match the short ends, with wrong sides together forming a loop. Stitch the seam, stretching to create the lettuce edge.
4. Finish both raw edges of the loop scarf, stretching as much as possible (be careful not to break your needle!) to get the fullest ruffled edge possible. Trim threads and go.

Side note: Create a skinny loop scarf with just one strip of the alternating color fleece pieces. Follow the same basic construction steps, but eliminate the second pieced strip before stitching into a loop. Layer two ruffled loop scarves on for added impact!

BASIC BEANIE

This classic cap comes in sizes to fit everyone in the family; babies, kids, and adults. Mix the cap and brim pieces to reflect your fave team colors, and add a tassel or pom-pom to top it off! We used a serger to whip ours together, making these super quick. Pair one with a matching scarf.

SUPPLIES

Pattern for Basic Beanie (page 143)
¼ yard, solid-color or team-print fleece
All-purpose sewing thread

CUT

Place pattern piece on fleece following the grain-line mark (stretch
   of fleece should be around head). Cut 4 hat pieces from fleece.
Cut a hat band: Baby 3" × 18", Child 4" × 20", Adult 5" × 24"
Set aside fleece scraps to make loop or tassel trim for top of hat if desired.

Note: Finished hat circumference: Baby 17", child 19", Adult 23".

1. With right sides together, match two hat body pieces, and stitch one side seam. Create two seamed "sets" of 2 from the 4 hat pieces.
2. Make tassel or loop and pin to top of one half of hat at upper edge of center seam on the right side, matching raw edges with trim towards the body of the hat. Baste in place to hold.
3. Place both hat halves right sides together and stitch remaining hat seam.
4. For band, place short ends right sides together and stitch seam. Fold band in half, wrong sides together, matching raw edges. Baste ⅛" from edge to keep layers from shifting.
5. Mark the band in quarters. Place band to hat raw edge, right sides together, matching quarter marks to seams. Stitch seam.

Tassel Top

Cut fleece scrap 2" wide x 3" tall. Along the 2" edge make 2"-deep cuts, spacing cuts ¼" apart to create fringe. Fold side edges to the center of the piece, making a 1" wide finished tassel. Baste to secure folds on unfringed end. Place basted end of tassel on top raw edge of cap, catching end in seam.

Loop Top

Cut fleece scrap ½" × 3". Fold in half. Catch raw ends in seam to form loop at top of hat.

FINGERLESS ARM WARMERS

We love gloves, but with all the tech gadgets we own, wearing a pair of fingerless arm warmers make it easier for us to be able to tweet updates at the game. Once you make one pair of these, you and your friends will want more, in all their favorite team colors.

SUPPLIES

Pattern for Fingerless Arm Warmers (page 143)

½ yard, solid-color fleece

½ yard, coordinating team-print fleece

½ yard, ⅝" matching fold-over elastic

All-purpose sewing thread

CUT

Place pattern piece on fleece, cut 2 each from solid-color fleece and
team-print fleece.

SEW

1. Layer each of the pieces, right sides together, with one solid piece to one print piece. Stitch inside seam, leaving a 2½" opening for your thumb as marked on the pattern.

2. Finger press this seam open. Top stitch ¼" on each side along the length of the seam, securing the seam edges.

3. With right sides together, stitch opposite seam.

4. Fold hem at finger end of arm warmer under 1", stitch close to raw edge with a narrow zigzag stitch (this hem will get a lot of stress, and needs to give).

5. Using fold-over elastic, starting at the inside seam of arm warmer, stitch elastic trim to sleeve opening. Match the wrong side of elastic to the raw edge of the wrong side of fabric (use the center line marking on the fold-over elastic as a guide to match the raw edge). Stitch with a 2.5 length-and-width zigzag stitch, lapping raw ends of the elastic on the inside seam of arm warmer.

6. Fold the elastic to the right side. Stitch close to the edge of the fold-over elastic using a straight stitch to secure.

EAR WARMER HEADBAND

Keep your hair in place and your ears covered with this fleece headband. Edged in fold-over elastic, the band even has a hole for your ponytail. The one-piece design makes it easy to work with team prints to get their logo in just the right position.

SUPPLIES:

Pattern for Ear Warmer Headband (page 144)
⅛ yard, solid-color or team-print fleece
1¼ yards, ⅝" matching fold-over elastic
All-purpose sewing thread

CUT

Place pattern piece on fold as marked, cut 1 from fleece.

SEW

1. Open ear warmer piece so it is one layer. Apply fold-over elastic to each long raw edge with a zigzag stitch, stretching the elastic slightly, with the wrong side of elastic to wrong side of ear warmer. (Use the center line marking on the fold-over elastic binding as a guide to match to raw edge.)
2. Fold the elastic trim to the right side, stitch close to the edge with a straight stitch to secure.
3. Match the raw ends, right side together, and stitch the seam, then finger press open.
4. Apply fold-over elastic to the ponytail opening using the same technique as step 1, starting at the lower side of the opening and lapping ends. Fold elastic trim to the right side and stitch to secure.

HOT HANDS MITTS

We know your hands can get cold in that stadium, and you need to sport your colors, too. Dilemma solved with these mitts that sport a pocket to hold those little warmer packets that keep your hands and fingers toasty. You can even stash a few tissues and a couple of bucks inside, too—the cord locks on the elastic drawstring will keep them snug on your hands while you are cheering wildly during the game.

SUPPLIES

Pattern for Hot Hands Mitts (page 144)

⅓ yard each, 2 coordinating team-print fleece

⅛ yard, ¾" hook-and-loop tape

1 yard, oval braided elastic

2 cord locks

Wash-away basting tape

All-purpose sewing thread

CUT

Place pattern piece for mitt on fleece, cut 2 each, of the 2 coordinating team-print fleeces.

Fold pattern piece along marking for mitt pocket, and place on team-print fleece, cut 2.

SEW

1. Cut hook-and-loop tape into 2, 2" pieces. Separate the hook pieces from the loop pieces. Place a piece of basting tape on the back of each piece, and remove cover to expose adhesive. Place loop piece on each pocket's hem edge, centering tape piece on hem with edge of tape next to raw edge of hem. Stitch around the edges of the tape to secure.
2. Turn up 1" hem on each pocket piece and stitch close to raw edge.
3. Attach the hook side of hook-and-loop tape pieces to the stitched loop tape. Layer the pocket pieces on 2 mitt pieces, with both pieces right side up. Press down on hook and loop tape to position hook piece on mitt piece. Carefully remove pocket piece and stitch tape onto each of the mitt pieces, stitching along tape edges.
4. Baste a pocket piece to each of the mitt pieces, with both pieces right side up, and matching raw edges.
5. Place each of the prepared mitt pieces and remaining mitt pieces right sides together, matching raw edges. On each mitt, opposite side seams (you will have a left and right mitt) stitch seam partially: Stitch 1" from lower edge, leave the next 1" unstitched, then stitch for an additional 3". Finger press seam allowances open and stitch close along both sides of seam, securing seam allowance to mitt.
6. Finish stitching the remaining mitt seam on each Hot Hands Mitt.
7. Turn under 1" hem to inside of each mitt. Stitch in place along hem raw edge.
8. Cut elastic into 2, 18" pieces. Thread elastic through casing and ends through a cord stop. Tie elastic ends together in an overhand knot, and trim ends.
9. Place hand warmer packets into pockets, slip mitts on, and adjust cord stop to fit wrists.

POM-POMS SPIRIT GLOVES

Our pom-pom gloves were created with black-and-white zebra-print fleece, achieving the blended look pictured. A team-print fleece will achieve a similar effect. Or, use two different color strips for each pom-pom for a two-toned pom-pom.

SUPPLIES	CUT
⅜ yard, team-print or solid-color fleece	Cut 22, ½" strips the full width of the fleece. It takes 2 strips to make each pom-pom.
1 pair of stretch gloves	Cut 2 of the ½" strips into 10, 12" pieces for tying the pom-poms.
Small pom-pom maker (Clover USA —optional)	
All-purpose sewing thread	

POM-POM MAKER: For each pom, use two strips of fleece. Wind 1 strip around each set of arms of the pom-pom maker. Fold the arms in, cut strips through the channel, tie with a 12" strip of fleece. Make 10 pom-poms.

POMS CREATED USING CARDBOARD TEMPLATE: Wind 2 strips around a 2" x 4" piece of cardboard the short way (wind around the 2" width). Thread the tie along one edge under the wound strips, pulling snug as you cut the strips across the opposite end to create pom-pom. Make 10 pom-poms.

SEW

1. Trim the tie ends on each of the poms to the same length as the pom "yarn" pieces. Trim each pom to shape if necessary to achieve a pleasing round pom-pom.
2. Tack a pom-pom to the fingertip of each glove (make sure you have a right and left glove!). Stitching through the tie ends of the pom-pom to attach, taking care to catch only one layer of each glove fingertip.
3. Repeat step 2 until all 10 pom-poms are attached.

POCKET PILLOW BLANKET

Is it a pillow or a blanket? Both! This generously sized fleece blanket can be folded up into a pocket. Flip the pocket over the blanket, fluff, and presto—you have a pillow. Easy to tote along or just keep on the couch to snuggle up with when game time rolls around.

SUPPLIES

2 yards, team-print fleece
½ yard, solid-color fleece
All-purpose sewing thread
Dinner plate or acrylic corner template for marking round corners

CUT

Trim selvedges from team-print fleece fabric (blanket) and straighten all edges.
Use template to mark and trim each of the corners to a rounded shape.
Cut 1, 16" × 18" rectangle from solid-color fleece (pocket).

SEW

1. On pocket piece, finish all edges with serger, if desired. With wrong sides facing, turn under 2" hem along a 16" side, to wrong side. Stitch to secure with a 2.5 length and width zigzag stitch.
2. Trim selvedges and straighten all edges of blanket piece. Finish all edges with serger, or fold under ½" hem all around and stitch to secure.
3. Fold blanket in half lengthwise. Mark center of blanket for placement of the pocket piece.
4. Place the hemmed pocket piece on the lower edge of blanket, matching left side of pocket piece to center mark and lower edge, wrong side of pocket to right side of blanket. Stitch ¼" away from the raw edges, leaving the hemmed upper edge free.
5. To fold blanket into the pocket to form the pillow, fold the blanket in half lengthwise, wrong sides together. Fold again lengthwise so that the pocket is still exposed. Place pocket side of folded blanket facedown, fold blanket up 3 folds (about 15" each time) towards the pocket. Then flip the pocket inside out over the folded blanket, adjusting the folds as necessary to form the pillow.

SNUGGLE COZY

Sleeves-on-a-blanket—this ingenious cover-up gives you the freedom to grab the remote (or the popcorn) while staying warm and snuggled up. While the snuggle cozy may look a bit unusual (okay, downright silly), once you try one you sure can't beat it for cold days in front of the TV!

SUPPLIES

2 yards, solid-color fleece (snuggle blanket)

⅔ yard, team-print fleece (sleeves and pocket)

All-purpose sewing thread

7" saucer or acrylic sleeve template for marking armholes

Trim selvedges from solid fleece (blanket) and straighten all edges.

Cut 2, 24" × 24" sleeves and 1, 10" × 15" rectangle for the pocket from team-print fleece.

SEW

1. Turn under 1" hem on all edges of blanket piece. Stitch hems close to raw edge to secure.
2. Mark the holes for the sleeves, using a 7" saucer or an acrylic sleeve template made just for a snuggly. With the hemmed blanket facing up, mark each opening 9" from both the upper and outside edges, one opening for each arm/sleeve. Trim along markings to create the openings.
3. Fold each sleeve piece, right sides together matching raw edges. Pin and stitch seam. Turn under a 1" hem on each sleeve, and stitch to secure.
4. Mark each sleeve opening on blanket in quarters and each of the sleeves along the raw edges in quarters. Set each sleeve, right sides together and pinning and matching the quarter marks, with each sleeve seam towards the lower portion of the blanket. Stitch seams.
5. Turn under 1" hem along the 15" upper edge of pocket piece and stitch to secure. Turn under ½" on remaining raw edges of pocket. Fold blanket in half lengthwise to find center. Mark center. Place pocket on blanket, right side up, matching center of pocket to center of blanket. Stitch ¼" from each of the pocket edges leaving hemmed upper edge free.

Optional: Create a pocket section to fit cell phone or remote by stitching a line from upper hem edge to pocket bottom, 4" from either end of finished pocket.

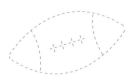

Two

Tailgate Party

PENNANT ANTENNA WARE

Slide this pennant onto your car antenna and your group will be easy to find in the vast sea of cars at your next tailgate get-together. A bit of polyester stuffing gives it some shape.

SUPPLIES

¼ yard, team-print fleece fabric
⅛ yard, coordinating solid-color fleece
Polyester fiberfill
Small pom-pom maker
All-purpose sewing thread

CUT

Cut 2, 8" × 11" triangles from team-print fleece for pennant pieces.
Cut 1, 2" × 12" strip and 2, ½" × 2" pieces from solid-color fleece (for binding and loops).
Cut 2, ½" × 60" strips from team-print fleece. Cut 2, ½" x 60" strips from solid-color fleece (for pom-poms).

SEW

1. Place pennant pieces right sides together. Stitch both long sides, leaving a 2" opening for stuffing. Trim corner and turn right side out.
2. Baste short edges of pennant closed.
3. Fold ½" x 2" strips in half crosswise, matching ends to make loops. Pin one at the top and one at the bottom corner of pennant, with the loop facing the body of the pennant. Baste in place.
4. Fold 2" x 12" strip in half lengthwise, sandwiching the raw edge of pennant into fold to bind. Stitch close to strip raw edge, through all layers. Stitch across upper edge of strip to close channel.
5. Make 2 pom-poms (See Pom-Pom Spirit Gloves, page 43). Tie one pom-pom onto each loop on the pennant.
6. Stuff pennant lightly with polyester fiberfill, just enough to give it some shape. Slip stitch opening closed. Slide over car antenna.

TABLE TOPPER THROW

Top your table with this super simple cover and when the partying is done bring it along to the game for a comfy lap throw. Even if there is a spill or two, fleece is virtually water repellant, so a couple of dabs should clean it right off!

SUPPLIES

1⅛ yards, team-print fleece
¼ yard, coordinating solid-color fleece
All-purpose sewing thread
Rotary cutter with straight and wave blades

CUT

Trim team-print fleece fabric to 40" square.
Using straight rotary blade on one edge and wave blade on opposite edge
   cut 4, 2" wide × 60" strips from solid-color fleece.

SEW

1. Measure 10" from each end of the 4 fleece strips, place a pin to mark.
2. Pin a fleece trim strip along one side of the fleece square, right sides up. Overlap straight edge of trim ½" over the raw edge of the fleece square (the wave edge is the decorative edge of the trim). Repeat until all 4 strips are pinned in place.
3. Stitch strips to topper, ¼" away from trim and strip raw edge, stopping 2" from each end of square (to allow room for tying ends).
4. Trim ends of each of the ties at an angle. At each corner tie loose ends into a square knot, positioning so the knot covers the corner neatly.

CASSEROLE CAP

This is kind of like a shower cap for your casserole, but from fleece! My mom used to have dish covers that were elasticized just like this, but we ramped up this style to give it the Game Day *touch*. The fleece cover has rip-stop nylon as the liner, so things stay nice and neat even after toting the dish to and from the party.

SUPPLIES

½ yard, team-print fleece

¼ yard, solid-color fleece

½ yard, rip-stop nylon

1 yard, ⅜" wide braided elastic

⅞ yard, 1" coordinating grosgrain ribbon

All-purpose sewing thread

Place your casserole dish facedown on the team-print fleece. Add ½" seam
  allowance all around. Cut fleece on this marking.

Cut same size piece for the lining from rip-stop nylon.

Measure around the outside of the rim of the casserole dish. Cut a strip of fleece,
  5" × perimeter of the casserole dish.

Cut 2, 15" pieces from grosgrain ribbon.

SEW

1. Place rip-stop nylon piece to wrong side of team-print fleece piece. Baste
   ⅜" from edges. Treat this as one piece.
2. Mark the outside edge of the lined fleece piece in quarters, starting in middle of one side edge (this is where the tie will be).
3. Fold solid-color fleece strip in half lengthwise, matching raw edges. Baste
   ⅜" from raw edges. Stitch ⅝" from folded edge creating casing. Mark the
   solid-color fleece strip in quarters.
4. Starting at the middle of one side, pin the fleece strip around the edge of the
   lined fleece piece. Place right sides together, match raw edges and quarter
   markings. The raw ends of the fleece strip will *meet* (but not overlap) at the
   center. Stitch seam.
5. Trim elastic to the same length as the fleece strip minus 6". Stitch ribbon
   ends to ends of the elastic. Thread drawstring through casing. Tie ribbon
   ends into bow and slip over casserole to cover.

CORN HOLE GAME

This is THE game for tailgate parties. What you may think is a Simple Simon game of bean bag toss soon turns into a down-and-dirty serious challenge—with your friends taking sides! This fun game can be played one-on-one or in pairs. Either way make the corn-filled bags and covers in your team colors, to coordinate with Corn Hole game boards that you can build yourself (see page 158).

Corn Hole Bags

SUPPLIES
1 yard, heavy duck cloth or canvas

1⅓ yards, ¾" hook-and-loop tape

Wash-away basting tape

All-purpose sewing thread

8 pounds of feed corn for filling bags (16 ounces for each bag)

CUT
Cut 8, 7" × 16" rectangle pieces from the canvas.

Cut hook-and-loop tape into 8, 6" strips.

SEW
1. Press under a 1" hem on both short ends of each canvas piece.
2. Place a strip of wash-away basting tape on the wrong side of each hook-and-loop strip. Remove protective cover to expose adhesive. Apply a hook strip on one end, and a loop strip on the opposite end of each canvas

piece. Center each strip along lower hem edge, ½" from each side edge. Stitch close to the long edge of each hook or loop strip, through all layers.

3. Fold each prepared bag in half, right sides together, matching sides. Stitch side seams. Double stitch each seam to reinforce.

4. Turn each bag right side out. Fill with 16 ounces of feed corn (measure on a scale to be precise!), then seal the corn bag using the hook-and-loop closure.

Corn Hole Covers

SUPPLIES

½ yard, 2 coordinating team-print or solid-color fleece
½ yard, ¾" wide hook-and-loop tape
Wash-away basting tape
All-purpose sewing thread

CUT

Cut 4, 7" × 16" rectangles from each of the 2 coordinating fleece pieces.
Cut hook-and-loop tape into 8, 2" strips.

SEW

1. On each fleece piece, turn under a 1" hem to the wrong side, on both short ends. Stitch close to hem raw edge to secure.

2. Place a strip of wash-away basting tape on the wrong side of each hook-and-loop strip. Remove protective cover to expose adhesive. Position a loop strip in the center of the hem, on one end of each of the fleece pieces. Stitch close to all edges of the tape, through all layers to secure.

3. Stitch a 2" hook strip on the opposite end of each fleece rectangle.

4. Position tape on right side of hemmed piece, centering 3½" from end. Stitch close to all edges of the tape, through all layers to secure.

5. Fold piece right sides together, overlapping ends, and secure hook-and-loop tape. Position of the inside hem edge is 4" from folded edge.

6. Stitch both side seams. Turn cover right side out and insert corn hole bags into the corn hole covers.

EASY-UP BANNER STRING

Personalizing your small parking space is part of the fun of any tailgate event. Make this banner string to hang from your pop-up awning or vehicle to add some style and mark your spot. Each of the banner pieces is cut from the team-print fleece fabric, leaving the cut edges as the finish. String 'em up and bring out the food!

SUPPLIES

¼ yard each, 2 coordinating team-print fleece

⅛ yard, solid-color fleece

2½ yards, ⅜" grosgrain ribbon

All-purpose sewing thread

CUT

Note: Take care to center team motifs on each piece before cutting.

Cut 3, 8" × 11" rectangles from team-print fleece.

Cut 2, 8" × 11" rectangles from coordinating team-print fleece.

Cut 1, 2½" × 60" strip from solid-color fleece fabric,

SEW

1. Trim rectangles to make 2 ribbon-shape pieces and 3 triangle-shape pieces as shown in the photo.
2. On the right side of each banner piece, mark a line 1" down from each upper edge. Cut a piece from the solid-color fleece strip the width of the upper edge of each banner piece, plus 1".
3. Along the line on the right side of the upper edge of each banner piece, place fleece strip right side up, extending strip ½" on each side. Pin in place, and stitch close to raw edge. Repeat for all 5 banner pieces.
4. Fold strip over the upper edge to the back side of each banner piece, creating the binding. Stitch on the front side, through all layers, ⅜" from raw edge, forming casing. Repeat for all 5 banner pieces. Trim any excess binding on each end of banner piece to neaten.
5. Using a safety pin, thread ribbon through casing on each banner, with right sides of all banners facing outwards. Adjust position of banners on ribbon evenly.

LACE-UP COFFEE COZY

Warm up those hands and keep the cup from getting too hot to handle with this slip-on coffee cozy. Laced up football style, it's a nod to the sport that made tailgating a national pastime.

SUPPLIES

Lace-up Coffee Cozy pattern (page 145)

⅛ yard, team-print fleece

⅛ yard, solid-color fleece

½ yard, cord elastic

8 eyelets

All-purpose sewing thread

CUT

Place pattern piece on fleece, taking care to position the print appropriately, cut 1 each, team-print and solid-color fleece.

Tip: Cut the solid color piece slightly larger—¼" beyond cut line, to make it easier to sew the layers.

SEW

1. Layer the two fleece pieces, with right sides facing up, and the solid-color piece on the bottom. Center the team-print piece and pin to hold. Stitch ⅛" from edge of the inset print piece, through both layers around all sides. Trim excess fleece close to stitching.
2. Mark placement for 5 eyelets on each end of piece, spacing evenly. Insert eyelets following instructions on package.
3. Lace elastic cord through eyelets, with laces crossing on inside of cozy, and straight across on the outside of finished cozy. On inside of cozy, tie the elastic cord ends into a double knot and trim away excess.
4. Slip finished Lace-Up Coffee Cozy over coffee cup until it fits snugly.

Three

Ladies Only

LADIES'
LAZY-DAY CAPRIS

Lounge around watching the game in style with these cuddly capris. Super easy to make, this one-piece pattern is a snap to whip together. The stretchy waist along with the adjustable tie makes these so comfy—even after all the snacks! Add sassy cuffs in a coordinating print to up their cute factor!

SUPPLIES

Commercial pajama pants pattern
Pattern paper
1½ yards, team-print fleece for pajama pants (see pattern)
½ yard, fleece animal-print fabric for cuff
1 package, ⅜" braided elastic
½ yard, ribbon or trim for pajama pant "ties"
All-purpose sewing thread

CUT

1. Lay out the pattern paper on a large surface.
2. Cut out the pant pattern size that you need. Lay the side seams overlapping,

matching the seam allowances, and tape to hold. Lay the adjusted pattern on pattern paper and trace. You now have your one-piece pattern. Cut the pattern to the desired length before adding contrast hem and cuff. We cut ours shorter for capris. You can also leave them long if you wish.

3. For the contrast cuff, on another piece of pattern paper redraw the bottom 6" of the pant pattern (after you have cut it to the length desired). Add a seam allowance to the top edge of the cuff pattern piece and mark the bottom of this piece to be placed on the fold of the fabric.

4. Pin the paper patterns for the pants and the contrast for the hem/cuff to the fleece. Cut two of each pattern piece.

SEW

1. Pin the front seam, right sides together. Stitch seam for 1", leaving a 1" unstitched space (to create opening for ties), then continue stitching the remainder of the seam. Be sure to lockstitch or backstitch to secure stitches.

2. Finger press seam open. Stitch the opened seam allowance close to the seam line, on both sides of the seam. Start at the upper waist edge, stitch down 2", securing the opened seam allowances to the capris. This will keep the seam allowance from folding over when the elastic is inserted.

3. Right sides together, pin the back seam and stitch seam.

4. Right sides together, front to back, pin the inside leg seams and stitch seam. Restitch this seam for extra strength.

5. Fold over 1" to the inside waist edge of the lounge pants. Stitch close to the raw edge, forming the casing.

6. Measure elastic to the waist, and subtract 6", cut elastic to this length. Cut 2 ties from the ribbon, each 9" long. Stitch a ribbon tie to each end of the elastic piece. Using a safety pin, thread the elastic tie through the casing. Adjust elastic so the fullness is evenly distributed. Tie the ribbon into a bow.

7. Right sides together, fold each cuff piece in half, matching raw edges. Stitch cuff side seam. Fold each cuff, wrong sides together, matching the raw edges. Baste edges through both layers to hold so layers won't shift.

8. Pin the contrast hem to the right side of the pant leg bottoms, matching the seams and raw edges of the fabric. Stitch right sides together. Turn up to form cuff. Tack stitch cuff in place on inside pant seam.

SHOW-ME SHRUG

A shrug is a timeless piece, and this one sports your favorite teams. Some girls wear their hearts on their sleeves . . . we show off our teams! Fleece "surgery" is an easy way to showcase your team logos, and the easy-on cover-up keeps the chills at bay. We stopped the sleeves at the elbow and added the animal print cuffs for a simple sleeve trim. Finish the remaining edges with fold-over elastic and you are off!

SUPPLIES

Show-Me Shrug Pattern (page 145)
1½ yards, solid-color fleece (shrug body)
¼ yard, coordinating animal-print cuddle fleece (cuffs)
Scraps of team-print fleece (motifs)
2½ yards, 1" matching fold-over elastic trim
All-purpose sewing thread

Using the pattern pieces, cut 2 separate front pieces and one back piece (with fabric positioned along the fold) from solid-color fleece. Cut two cuffs from cuddle fleece, 6" × 14".

From team-print fleece, cut two motifs, trimming ½" outside the perimeter of the design that will be stitched on. Cut one motif for each sleeve.

SEW

1. Stitch each trimmed motif to right side of the front sleeve area, approximately 1" from lower edge of sleeve. Pin in place then stitch ¼" away from edge, creating applique. Trim close to stitching as necessary.

2. Place shrug pieces, right sides together, matching shoulder seams. Stitch and finger press seam open.

3. With right sides together, match underarm seams. Stitch seam. Finger press seam open.

4. Create two cuffs from the cuddle fleece fabric pieces. Fold each rectangle, right sides together, matching the 6" ends. Stitch seam. Fold in half, wrong sides together, forming cuff. Baste upper raw edges together ⅜" from edge to keep fabric from shifting.

5. Match prepared cuff at sleeve opening, right sides together, matching seam in cuff to underarm seam. Stitch seam. Finger press seam towards body of shrug.

6. Finish the outside edges of the shrug with fold-over elastic binding. Starting at the side seam, match the wrong side of the fold-over elastic to the raw edge of the wrong side of fabric (use the center line marking on the fold-over elastic as a guide to match the raw edge). Stretch the elastic slightly as you are applying it. Stitch through elastic edge and fleece using a 2.5 length and width zigzag stitch, lapping raw ends of the elastic at the side seam.

7. Fold the elastic to the right side. Stitch close to the edge of the fold-over elastic using a straight stitch to secure.

CUDDLE SCARF—MINI

This really is just a simple rectangle, with the lower edge finished and elastic at the upper edge to pull it into the cowl shape. Add your logo cutouts—one team on the front and the other on the back for dual wear. Bonus: the Cuddle Scarf-Mini makes an uber-cute mini-skirt when paired with tights.

SUPPLIES

½ yard, print cuddle fleece

⅔ yard, ⅜" braided elastic

Scraps of 2 team-print fleece (motifs)

All-purpose sewing thread

CUT

Cut 1, 18" × 40" rectangle from print cuddle fleece.

Cut two motifs per team, from each team-print fleece, trimming ½" outside the perimeter of the design.

SEW

1. With right sides together matching 18" sides, fold cuddle fleece rectangle. Stitch seam. Finger press open. Turn right side out.
2. Turn under ½" along both unfinished edges, forming hem at bottom and casing at upper edge. Stitch hem to secure. Stitch casing close to edge, leaving 2" opening for elastic.
3. Mark finished hem edge of cuddle in quarters. Lay out so that seam is along one side and fold is along the other, and centers are matched. Position trimmed motifs at center of each side of cuddle fleece fabric, spacing motifs as desired (ours were 1" from lower edge and about 6" from upper edge on front and back). Pin in place then stitch ¼" away from edge, creating applique. Trim close to stitching as necessary.
4. Using a safety pin, thread elastic through casing. Overlap elastic ends and stitch. Stitch casing opening closed. Adjust elastic to evenly distribute fullness.

Note: Wear as a cuddle cowl scarf with your best team facing forward and gathered edge at neck. Or, as a mini, with the seam towards the back.

THE COVERUP

This is our quick take on a garment bag, but without the hassle of a zipper. Just take your clothes that are on the hanger, pop this open-bottom cover over your clothes, and you are out the door. A little whipstitched fleece trim adds just the right amount of finesse. Ours is "suit length," but if you want to make it a little longer just add a few inches to the bottom edge. Easy-peasy!

Finished size: 22" × 34"

SUPPLIES

1 yard, team-print fleece (Print #1 for main body)

½ yard, coordinating team-print fleece (Print #2 for upper section)

⅛ yard, solid-color fleece (trim)

3½ yards, ¼" satin ribbon

All-purpose sewing thread

Wood hanger

CUT

From print #1: Cut 1, 23" × 36" rectangle for the back, and 1, 23" × 22" rectangle for the lower front.

From print #2: cut 1, 23" × 15" rectangle for the upper front.

From solid-color fleece: cut 1, 1¼" x 60" strip width of the fleece.

1. Right sides together, stitch upper front piece to lower front piece, along 23" side, positioning prints so they are both right side up after seam is sewn. Finger press seam open.

2. Right sides together, place the assembled front to the back, matching all raw edges. Take care that the team prints on each piece are facing in the correct direction. Mark center of the upper edge of the 23" side of rectangle, then mark 2" on each side of center to mark a 4" hanger opening. Place wooden hanger at center mark, with hanger body on fabric and hanger hook above fabric edge. Mark slope, following edge of hanger. Trim away excess fabric along marking, through both layers.

3. Cut long fleece strip into 1, 24" piece and 2, 12" pieces. Mark holes for ribbon spacing 1" apart and ¼" away from raw edge, on both sides of each fleece strip. Use a small-tip awl (such as the one that comes with your sewing machine for buttonholes) to make holes for the ribbon, or use a sharp-point tapestry needle to prepunch the holes, following the spaced markings. Whip stitch the narrow ribbon through the holes, using a blunt-point tapestry needle, adjusting the ribbon as necessary to keep a flat, smooth look. Leave at least 1" extra ribbon on the ends of all of the pieces.

4. Stitch across the short ends of the embellished strip to secure ribbons. Right sides up, position the long 24" embellished strip on the right side of the cover front, overlapping the seam. Stitch along both edges, close to ribbon stitches, attaching trim to front.

5. Fold remaining short embellished strips into a loop, matching raw ends. Hand tack ends together on each loop. Layer the loops on top of each other, with the raw ends to the underside, angling loops slightly to form a bow. Tack through center to hold. Use a button or small fleece loop at center of bow to finish. Hand stitch bow to cover front, along trim piece, 8" from side edge. (Here we made a contrasing bow.)

6. Place embellished front cover to back cover piece, right sides together, matching raw edges. Stitch side seams to upper opening. Leave upper opening free for hanger. Turn cover right side out.

7. Turn in ½" hem at upper opening. Stitch hem to secure.

8. Turn up 1" hem at lower edge to the inside of cover. Slip in hanger(s) and go!

RAIN-DELAY BOOT LINERS

Rain boots are pretty much a staple in all of our wardrobes, and while they are really practical they certainly aren't very warm. No more need to layer on the tube socks—just make a pair of these to line your galoshes. And since they are stirrup style you can still wear your own team socks.

SUPPLIES

Rain-Delay Boot Liners pattern (page 145)

⅜ yard, team-print fleece (liner)

¼ yard, coordinating animal-print (cuff)

⅜ yard, ¾" braided elastic

All-purpose sewing thread

CUT

Using the pattern cut 4 boot liner pieces (2 for right boot and 2 for left boot) from the team-print fleece.

Cut 2 cuff pieces 8" × 17" from the animal-print fleece.

Cut two motifs from the team-print fleece, one each to be placed on the outside cuff of the boot liners, trimming ½" outside the perimeter of the design that will be stitched on.

SEW

1. Place 2 boot liner pieces right sides together. Stitch the inside and outside leg seams. Repeat for other liner.
2. Turn up ½" hem on the small lower edge of each liner. Stitch hem to secure using a 2.5 width and length zig-zag stitch.
3. Mark the center of each lower finished edge of liner for placement of the elastic stirrup. Cut elastic into 2, 7" pieces. Match ends of elastic to the center marks, overlapping ½". Adjust elastic as needed to fit. Stitch through elastic and hem to secure. Stitch each end twice for reinforcement, as the stirrups will get a lot of stress.
4. Right sides together, match 8" ends of cuff pieces. Stitch seam. Fold piece wrong sides together, raw edges matching, forming cuff. Baste to hold layers from shifting.
5. Stitch motifs onto cuff. Find and mark folded edge, the motif is to be stitched on so it is right side up when cuff is folded down on the outside of your boots!
6. Match raw edge of each cuff to each boot liner upper edge, right side of cuff to the wrong side of the boot liner (this cuff will flip from the inside of liner over to the outside of liner, forming the finished cuff), with the seam at the back leg seam of each liner. Stitch seams. Turn cuffs to right side of each boot liner.

Note: You can cut the body of the boot liner pieces shorter or longer as needed to fit your specific boots.

FLOWER POWER HEADWRAP

Is it a headband or an ear warmer? Actually both! This headwrap is the perfect cover for when you want to keep your ears toasty warm without that dreaded helmet hair! We made the band wide to cover your head and ears, and skinny in the back so it will lie at the nape of the neck like a headband.

SUPPLIES

Flower Power Headwrap pattern
   (pg. 145)
¼ yard, team-print cuddle fleece
¼ yard, animal-print cuddle fleece
   (lining)
⅛ yard, solid-color fleece (flower)
2", ¾" braided elastic
All-purpose sewing thread
Antique button for flower trim
Jewelry pin back
Fabric glue

CUT

Using pattern piece, cut 1 each from
   team-print cuddle fleece and
   animal-print cuddle fleece.
Cut 1, 1½" × 30" strip from
   solid-color fleece.

SEW

1. Right sides together, match edges of team-print headwrap piece. Stitch seams along both long sides. Leave ends open. Turn headwrap right side out.
2. Tuck in raw ends ½" at each end of headwrap. Slip elastic piece into each open end and stitch in place, to catch. Stitch over same stitches to reinforce.

Flower Pin
See page 77 for Flower Pins.

FLOWER POWER SCARF

Removable fleece flowers amp up the glam on this simple scarf. And it's all straight sewing—no curves ahead! We color blocked the ends to add some interest and show off the rhinestone trimmed blossoms. Add the matching Flower Power Headwrap for those head-turning "look at me" glances!

SUPPLIES

 ¼ yard, team-print fleece (scarf)
 ¼ yard, animal-print cuddle fleece (trim)
 ⅛ yard, solid-color coordinating fleece (flowers)
 All-purpose sewing thread

Fabric glue

Jewelry pin backs

Buttons, pearls, and 20mm flatback rhinestones for flower embellishment

CUT

Trim and straighten team-print fleece fabric to 9" × 60."

Cut 2, 9" × 6" rectangles from cuddle fleece fabric.

Cut 2, 1½" × 30" strips solid-color fleece.

SEW

Scarf

1. Right sides together, place animal-print cuddle fleece pieces on each end of long printed fleece piece, matching 9" sides. Stitch seams. Finger press seams open.
2. With right sides together and long edges matching, stitch each end and long seam to center of scarf, leaving a 4" opening for turning. Clip corners to reduce the bulk. Turn right side out. Slip stitch opening closed.

Flower Pins

1. With shears, round end of each long strip. Gather each long strip by hand using a running stitch, spacing stitches ¼" apart. Gather each strip tight to 6", knot threads to secure.
2. Roll up the gathered strip, with raw gathered edge forming bottom of flower. Pin to hold through the layers. Stab stitch through bottom layers several times, crossing stitches across bottom of flower. Knot threads. Trim a quarter-size round piece of fleece from solid scraps. Glue to bottom of flower to create a flat surface to which to glue pin back. Allow glue to dry.
3. Embellish flowers with a large pearl button glued in the center of one fleece flower, and glue 20mm flatback rhinestones in a scattered pattern to the "petals" of the second flower. Allow glue to dry.
4. Attach pin back to each fleece flower using a generous amount of fabric glue. Let dry. Open pin back and apply a thin bead of glue to inside of pin back to help it hold securely. Let glue dry. Pin flowers to each end of the scarf.

Four

Man Cave

MENS LAZY-DAY
LOUNGE PANTS

Guys get in the game, too, with these comfy lounge pants. Basic design and assembly is the same as all the loungers in this book, and features the popular stretchy drawstring waist. A side pocket sports a fleece "surgery" logo and is an ample size to hold the remote for hands-free cheering (or booing).

SUPPLIES

Commercial pajama pants pattern (to make into a one-piece pattern)
Pattern paper
Team-print fleece, yardage to fit prepared pattern piece
¼ yard, coordinating solid-color fleece (pockets)
Scrap of team-print fleece for fleece "surgery" logo
½ yard, ⅜" twill tape (ties at waist)
1 package, ⅜" braided elastic
All-purpose sewing thread

CUT

Steps for cutting are the same as with Ladies' Lazy-Day Capris (pages 64–65). Cut 1, 9" × 10" pocket from solid-color fleece.

SEW

1. Right sides together, pin the front seam. Stitch seam for 1", leave a 1" unstitched space (to create opening for ties), then continue stitching the remaining seam. Be sure to use lockstitch or backstitch to secure stitches.
2. Finger press seam open. Stitch the opened seam allowance close to the seam line, on both sides of the seam. Starting at the upper waist edge, stitch down 2", securing the opened seam allowances to the lounge pants. This will keep the seam allowance from folding over when the elastic is inserted.
3. On left pants leg and centering pocket on pant leg, measure placement for pocket, 12" down from upper waist edge. Along upper edge of pocket, turn under 1" hem to wrong side. Pin in place and stitch close to raw edge, securing hem. Trim fleece motif to ½" away from logo. Center logo on pocket, stitch ¼" away from raw edge, trim excess close to stitching as needed. Place prepared pocket on right side of left pant leg, matching placement markings, right side up. Stitch ¼" away from unfinished edges, leaving upper hemmed edge free. Reinforce stitching at upper pocket edges as this will get a lot of stress.
4. Right sides together, match and pin back seam. Stitch seam.
5. Right sides together, pin the inside leg seams, front to back. Stitch seam. Restitch this seam for extra strength.
6. Fold over 1" to the inside waist edge of the lounge pants. Stitch close to the raw edge, forming the casing.
7. Turn under 1" hem to inside on each pant leg. Stitch close to the raw edge on each hem.
8. Measure waist. Cut elastic for waist, less 6". Stitch ribbon ties to each end of the waistline elastic piece. Using a safety pin, insert drawstring into the waist through the casing opening. Adjust elastic fullness and tie ribbon ends together.

CAN SLEEVE

Drink up with this sporty can cover. Cut the logo fleece so that the design is featured, and then stitch it up in a flash. Make several, because all the guys will want their own. And don't be surprised if they tend to "walk away" after the game is over!

SUPPLIES

¼ yard, solid-color fleece (can sleeve lining)

⅛ yard, coordinating team-print fleece (can sleeve motif)

3½", ⅜" braided elastic

All-purpose sewing thread

CUT

Cut 1, 5" × 9" rectangle from solid-color fleece

Cut 1, 4" × 9" rectangle from coordinating team-print fleece. Take care to center or adjust placement of the team motif as desired before cutting.

SEW

1. Right sides facing up, center the smaller fleece rectangle on top of larger rectangle. Using a 2.5 width and length zigzag stitch, sew over the raw edge of the smaller rectangle. Secure all edges to base piece.
2. Trim the larger piece with a rotary cutter, exactly ¼" beyond the zigzag stitching, around all edges.
3. On the wrong side of the lower edge mark placement for the elastic. Measure 2" in from each side edge, pin each end of the 3 ½"-long piece of elastic at these markings. Stitch through the elastic along lower edge using the zigzag stitching as a guide for placement, stretching the elastic as you go.
4. Right sides together, fold can sleeve in half. Match short ends and stitch seam. Finger press seam open. Tack seam open at the upper and lower edges following the original zigzag stitching, concealing the stitching.
5. Slip in can. Bottoms up!

BOTTLE BAG

Similar to the Can Sleeve, but made to fit a longneck bottle. Narrow elastic helps to shape the bag to the bottle, add a cord lock to make switching the drinks out easy. Bonus—fleece acts as an insulator to help keep drinks cold and hands dry.

SUPPLIES

¼ yard, team-print fleece

3½", ⅜" braided elastic

12" oval elastic for drawstring

Cord lock

All-purpose sewing thread

CUT

From the team-print fleece cut 1, 9" (wide) × 8" (tall) rectangle.

SEW

1. Right sides together, fold fleece rectangle in half, matching 8" sides. Stitch seam ½" down from top edge, leave a ½" opening unstitched, then continue to stitch rest of the seam. Be sure to lockstitch or backstitch to secure stitching.
2. Turn under ½" hem at the upper and lower edges of seamed piece. Stitch hems close to edge to secure.
3. Place seamed and hemmed piece on flat surface with seam at one side. On the wrong side of the lower edge mark placement for the elastic at seam line and opposite folded edge. Pin each end of the 3½" long piece of elastic at these markings. Stitch through the elastic along the lower edge using hem stitch line as a guide, stretching the elastic as you go.
4. Thread the oval elastic through the upper casing. Bring ends of elastic together and slip through cord lock. Knot elastic ends to keep cord lock from slipping off.
5. Insert beverage bottle into bag, draw cord up, and snug tight with cord lock.

T-SHIRT MEMORY BLANKET AND FLOOR PILLOW

Our speed demon method for creating a T-shirt blanket. Fleece borders frame each T-shirt, and the pieced top is backed with a coordinating team-print fleece. And for those T-shirts that did not make the first cut, perform some T-shirt surgery on the coveted logos to create a coordinating floor pillow.

Blanket

SUPPLIES

9 logo-imprinted T-shirts

1½ yards, solid-color fleece (sashing)

1¾ yards, team-print fleece (back)

7 yards, fusible knit interfacing

Acrylic fringe-cut ruler

Rotary cutter and mat

All-purpose sewing thread

CUT

Cut 6, 3" x 15" strips, 2, 3" x 47" strips, 2, 7½" x 47" strips, and 2, 7½" x 60" strips from solid-color fleece

Cut 1, 60" x 60" square from team-print fleece

Cut 9, 15" x 15" squares, 6, 3" x 15" strips, 4, 3" x 47" strips, and 2, 3" x 60" strips from fusible knit interfacing

On each T-shirt, mark a 15" square, positioning the imprinted logo where desired for each of the blocks. Cut squares from each T-shirt, leaving 1" all around beyond markings. Set T-shirt scraps aside for the floor pillow.

PREP

On each T-shirt block, mark the corners of the 15" square with pins. Using pin marks, place a fusible interfacing square on the wrong side of the T-shirt block. Following manufacturer's instructions, fuse the interfacing, taking care not to melt the imprint on the tee. A nonstick pressing sheet comes in handy for keeping the T-shirt from sticking to the ironing board!

On each of the 3" solid-color fleece strip, fuse the matching-size knit interfacing strip to the wrong side of the fleece strip. On the 4 remaining 7½" solid-color fleece strips, fuse the 3" strip of knit interfacing along one long edge.

SEW

1. Lay all the interfaced T-shirt blocks in a pattern as desired for the finished blanket, 3 blocks wide × 3 blocks high. Make note of each block position for your sewing order.

2. Create 3 rows of T-shirt blocks connected with fleece sashing pieces between. Stitch a 3" × 15" fleece strip to the right-facing edge of a T-shirt block, right sides together, then attach the next T-shirt block (per your layout) to the fleece strip, right sides together. Continue attaching a 3" × 15" fleece strip to that T-shirt block, and attach the last T-shirt block in the row, right sides together, to the fleece strip. Your pieced T-shirt row should be T-shirt block, 3" fleece strip, T-shirt block, 3" fleece strip, T-shirt block. Repeat with the remaining T-shirt blocks and strips to create 3 rows.

3. Lay the pieced T-shirt rows on a flat surface, again positioning as desired for the finished blanket. Right sides together, stitch a 3" × 47" fleece strip to the lower edge of the top row as sashing. Continue, attaching the next pieced row, right sides together, top of this row edge to lower edge of the 3" × 47" strip. Repeat, attaching the remaining 3" strip as sashing, then the last row. Your pieced T-shirt blanket top should have 3 rows of pieced T-shirt strips with 2 rows of fleece sashing between each of the rows.

4. Right sides together, attach the 7½" × 47" fleece strips to the upper and lower edges of the pieced T-shirt blanket top, placing the interfaced edge towards the blanket top.

5. Right sides together, attach the 7½" × 60" fleece strips to each long side

of the pieced T-shirt blanket top, placing the interfaced edge towards the blanket top.

6. Lay the trimmed team-print fleece fabric blanket back wrong side up on a large flat surface. Wrong sides together, place the pieced T-shirt blanket top on the team-print fleece, matching the raw edges all around.

7. Mark 4" in from raw edges on all sides, creating a line as a guide for fringe.

8. Following the 4" markings that overlap at the corners, trim away corners through both fleece layers. With an acrylic fringe-cut ruler as a guide, cut 1"-wide fringe strips up to the 4" mark through both fleece layers using a rotary cutter. Continue cutting fringe on one side of blanket until entire edge is fringed. If you do not have an acrylic fringe cut ruler and a rotary cutter, you can use a sharp pair of shears and a 1" ruler as a guide for making even fringe cuts.

9. With both layers together, tie each of the fringe strips into an overhand knot. Continue knotting fringe, taking care to keep knots in alignment and even along the pillow edge. Complete the fringe knots on one edge, then rotate pillow layers and repeat from step 8 until all sides are complete.

Pillow

Following instructions above, create 4 T-shirt or fleece blocks for the pillow top. Piece the fleece and T-shirt blocks together using the 3" wide fleece sashing between the T-shirt and embellished fleece blocks, and 3" sashing along the outside edges. From team-print fleece, cut out backing using the pillow top as a guide. Place pillow top and back right sides together, stitch all sides ½" from edges, leaving 4" opening for stuffing. Turn pillow right side out, stuff with polyester fiberfill. Stitch opening closed.

Five

Rookies

GIRLS' LAZY-DAY CAPRIS

Girls just want to have fun and lounge around in style too! These pj cuties are capris length, with a snazzy band and bow at the hem, with the same easy-to-sew waist as all of our Game Day loungers.

SUPPLIES

Commercial pajama pants pattern (to make into a one-piece pattern)

Pattern paper

Team-print fleece, yardage to fit prepared pattern piece

¼ yard, solid-color fleece (bands)

½ yard, ⅜" grosgrain ribbon (bows on bands)

½ yard, 1" satin ribbon (ties at waist)

¾ yard, ⅜" braided elastic

All-purpose sewing thread

Steps for cutting are the same as Ladies' Lazy-Day Capris (pages 64–65).
Cut strips for bands 3" wide.

SEW

1. Right sides together, pin the front seam. Stitch seam 1", leave a 1" unstitched space (to create opening for ties), then continue stitching the remaining seam. Be sure to lockstitch or backstitch to secure stitches.

2. Finger press seam open. Stitch the opened seam allowance close to the seam line on both sides of the seam. Start at the upper waist edge and stitch down 2", securing the opened seam allowances to the capris. This will keep the seam allowance from folding over when the elastic is inserted.

3. Right sides together, pin the back seam and stitch seam.

4. Right sides together, front to back, pin the inside leg seams. Stitch seam. Restitch this seam for extra strength.

5. Make bands for the hem finish. Right sides together, stitch short ends of fleece strips. Wrong sides together, fold each fleece loop in half lengthwise, matching raw edges. Baste ⅜" away from edges, through both layers, to prevent layers from shifting. Right sides together, place band on lower hem edge of each leg, matching seams. Stitch seam. Finger press seam towards the leg. Make two bows from the ⅜" ribbon. Hand tack bows at outside of legs, along the band.

6. Fold over 1" on the waist edge. Stitch close to the raw edge, forming the casing.

7. Measure waist. Cut elastic for waist, less 4". Stitch ribbon ties to each end of the elastic. Using a safety pin, insert elastic into the waist through the casing opening. Adjust fullness and tie ribbon ends into a bow.

FRINGY SPIRIT BOA

Everybody we know makes these fringy scarves from fleece to match their school and team colors. As long as you can do a zigzag stitch on your machine (even if you can't sew perfectly straight!) you can make these by the dozens. Don't even try to make just one . . . they are so easy and fast you might as well make them for the whole team.

SUPPLIES

¼ yard each, 3 coordinating team-print or solid-color fleece

All-purpose sewing thread

Acrylic fringe-cut ruler

Rotary cutter and mat

CUT

Kids' Boa: Cut each fabric piece to 6" × 48"

Adult Boa: Cut each fabric piece to 8" × 60"

SEW

1. With the 2 outside layers facing right side out, layer all three strips. Pin to hold layers in place. Use a few safety pins in addition to straight pins to hold.
2. Find the center of the layered strip (3" from edge for kids' boa, 4" for adult boa). Mark a line down the length of the strip.
3. Following the center line, stitch through all three layers using a narrow 1.0 wide and 3.0 long zigzag stitch. Remove pins and safety pins as you stitch, taking care that layers do not shift during sewing.
4. Trim ends to neaten. Reinforce stitching at the ends to keep boa layers secure.
5. With an acrylic fringe-cut ruler as a guide, cut ½" wide strips through all 3 fleece layers with rotary cutter, to ½" from center stitching. Continue cutting strips until both sides of boa are fringed. Take care not to cut through stitching. If you do not have an acrylic fringe-cut ruler and a rotary cutter, you can use a sharp pair of shears and a ruler to mark the ½" fringe.
6. Shake to settle fringe into boa.

BOYS' LAZY-DAY LOUNGE PANTS

Rough-and-tumble boys love to wear these lounge pants just as much as sweet and sassy girls practically live in theirs. For the little guys, we cut them long like the big dudes, and added a contrast, shaped pocket on the hip for stashing whatever their heart desires. Just remember to empty the pockets before washing—you never know what's hiding!

SUPPLIES

Pattern paper

Commercial pajama pants pattern (to make into a one-piece pattern)

Solid-color fleece, yardage to fit prepared pattern piece

⅜ yard, coordinating solid-color fleece fabric (pockets)

½ yard, ⅜" grosgrain ribbon (ties at waist)

¾ yard, ⅜" braided elastic

All-purpose sewing thread

Steps for cutting are the same as for Ladies' Lazy-Day Capris (pages 64–65)
Cut 2 pockets using a dinner plate for marking a circle shape.

SEW

1. Right sides together, pin the front seam. Stitch seam 1", leave a 1" unstitched space (to create opening for ties), then continue stitching the remaining seam. Be sure to lockstitch or backstitch to secure stitches.
2. Finger press seam open. Stitch the opened seam allowance close to the seam line on both sides of the seam. Start at the upper waist edge and stitch down 2", securing the opened seam allowances to the pants. This will keep the seam allowance from folding over when the elastic is inserted.
3. On each pant leg and centered on pant leg, measure placement for pockets, 10" down from upper waist edge. Fold each fleece pocket circle down 2" to right side, creating pocket flap. Stitch through the center of the circle, catching flap. Place each pocket on placement markings and stitch around outside edge of each pocket ¼" away from row edge. Reinforce backstitch at upper pocket edges as these will get a lot of stress.
4. Right sides together, match and pin back seam and stitch seam.
5. Right sides together and front to back, pin the inside leg seams. Stitch seam. Restitch this seam for extra strength.
6. Fold over 1" to the inside waist edge. Stitch close to the raw edge, forming the casing.
7. Turn under 1" hem on each leg. Stitch close to the raw edge on each hem.
8. Measure waist. Cut elastic for waist less 4". Stitch ribbon ties to each end of the elastic. Using a safety pin, insert elastic into the waist through the casing opening. Adjust fullness and tie ribbon ends together.

NAP PAD PILLOW BUDDY

Tote this naptime pal for your little one's very own sleepy time spot. Curtail the struggle with a cranky child, knowing they can rest at home, at the sitter's, at Grandma's, or even in the backseat of the car. The cover fits over a standard inexpensive preschool nap mat, and has a built-in pillow. When you are ready to go, just fold it up and tie.

SUPPLIES

⅝ yard each, 2 coordinating solid-color fleece

1⅜ yards, ⅜" grosgrain ribbon

1 small bag of polyester fiberfill

6 inch, ¾" hook-and-loop tape

All-purpose sewing thread

Kindergarten nap mat

CUT

Cut 1, 20" × 60" rectangle from each of the 2 fleece pieces

SEW

1. Turn under 1" hem on one short end of each fleece rectangle piece. Stitch hem to secure.
2. Cut hook-and-loop tape into 3, 2 inch pieces. Place 3 hook pieces along the wrong side of one finished edge of fleece rectangle, placing one piece in center and the other 2 pieces 1" in from each raw edge. Stitch in place around edge of tape pieces to secure. Stitch the 3 loop pieces along the finished edge of the remaining fleece piece in the same manner.
3. With right sides together, matching finished edges, stitch side seams and unfinished end.
4. Turn right side out and finger press along edges. Stitch pillow section 12" from closed end of cover, leaving a 3" opening in the center for stuffing. Stitch the ribbon tie at center, on upper edge of pillow section, through center of ribbon tie.
5. Stuff the pillow section with polyester fiberfill. Push stuffing away from opening and stitch opening closed. Insert mat into cover. Close hook-and-loop tape.
6. To store, fold accordion style, and tie ribbon around pad.

BRAIDS BEANIE

Take our basic beanie cap, add braids and ear covers . . . presto, instant Braids Beanie! Left loose, the braided ties add just the right amount of kitschy cuteness, along with that boho touch to Game Day outerwear.

SUPPLIES

Basic Beanie (page 143) and Braids Beanie pattern (earflaps) (page 147)

¼ yard, solid-color fleece (hat and braid)

⅛ yard, contrast solid-color fleece (band, flaps. and braid)

All-purpose sewing thread

Using Basic Beanie pattern, cut 4 pieces from solid-color fleece. Using the Braids Beanie pattern, cut 1, 3" × 19" band and 4 ear flaps from the contrast-color fleece.

Cut 1" × 15" strips for braid ties: 4 solid-color fleece, 2 contrast-color fleece, (6 ties—3 for each braid).

Cut 1, ½ inch wide strip for pom-pom, 60" long from each solid-color fleece.

SEW

1–5. Follow Steps 1 through 5 for Basic Beanie.

6. Using the 1" × 15" fleece strips, create braid ties. Group 3 strips together, 2 of main color and 1 of contrast. Baste one end of the set of 3 to hold strips together. Braid the strips to 4" from end. Knot end of braid, trim ends of fleece strips to neaten.

7. Place the unfinished end of each braid tie on the pointed end of each earflap piece, with the braid facing up toward the straight upper flap edge. Baste to hold braid in place. Match remaining earflap pieces to prepared earflap pieces, right sides together, sandwiching the braid between the two pieces. Stitch along earflap on edges, catching in braid tie, leaving upper flap edges unstitched. Turn earflaps right side out, match upper edges and baste ¼" from raw edge to secure.

8. With the band folded up towards the hat, match each earflap to the band seam of the hat, on the right side of hat. Matching raw edges, center earflaps over each hat section on opposite sides of the hat. Stitch seam through all fleece layers. Fold band and earflaps down so that braid ties extend.

9. Make pom-pom as for Pom-Poms Spirit Gloves (page 43) using the 2 fleece strips. Tack finished pom-pom to the top of the hat.

YO-YO FLOWERS SCARF

Fleece yo-yos as flowers add a playful element to this color-blocked scarf. Pair it up with the Braids Beanie for a duo that little girls will love to show off. And the simple pieced scarf, sans yo-yos, can showcase colors and team logos with easy style.

SUPPLIES

¼ yard each, 2 coordinating solid-color fleece
Extra-large yo-yo maker
Decorative buttons
All-purpose sewing thread

CUT

Cut 1, 6" × 48" strip from each of the 2 fleece pieces.

SEW

1. Place both long fleece strips right sides together and raw edges matching. Stitch both long seams, leaving a 4" opening along one side, for turning.
2. On each end of the scarf, position seams so that they are offset 2" (there will be a wide and a narrow strip of color opposite on each side of scarf). Matching raw edges, pin and stitch seams at each end.
3. Turn scarf right side out. Slip stitch opening closed.
4. Create fleece yo-yos following the instructions on page 23. Make 2 yo-yos from each of the 2 colors of fleece. Place a decorative button in the center of each and stitch in place.
5. Mark placement for yo-yos close to ends of the scarf, on top of the intersection of the seams. Place one of each color side by side. Tack in place around the outside edges taking care to stitch through one layer of the scarf so the stitches will not show on the back side of the scarf.

Six

Littlest Fan

REVERSIBLE PULLOVER BIB

The water-resistant properties of fleece sure come in handy on this reversible fleece bib to keep the inevitable spills and dribbles from soaking through. A stretch Lycra binding is soft against delicate baby's skin, and pulls over the head with no fasteners to mess with. And if one side gets a little unsightly, flip it over—ta-da—ready for the game and company!

SUPPLIES
Pattern for Reversible Pullover Bib (page 148)

⅓ yard each, 2 team-print fleece

⅛ yard, Lycra spandex fabric

All-purpose sewing thread

CUT
Using the Reversible Pullover Bib pattern, cut 1 bib from each team-print fleece.

Cut 1, 1½" × 16" strip from Lycra spandex fabric for neck trim.

SEW
1. Place both bib pieces right sides together, matching raw edges. Stitch seam, then turn right side out. Topstitch ½" around bib edge.
2. Match neck hole edges, and baste ¼" from edge.
3. Right sides together, starting at the back neck of the bib, place spandex strip onto neckline edge. Pin in place, stretching strip evenly around neckline, overlapping end ½" at back neck. Stitch ⅜" from neck edge.
4. Fold spandex strip to the underside of the bib, snug over the raw edge. Pin binding evenly in place, then stitch in the ditch on the front side of bib (the point where the spandex meets the fleece) to secure the binding while hiding the stitches. Trim excess binding close to stitching.

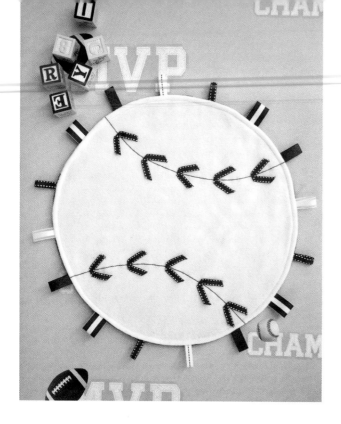

TAGGLES LOVEY

We have been spotting these loopy ribbon-edged mini blankets everywhere. Call it a lovey or a blankie, whatever name you like! Ours is a nod to baseball with dual sides—baseball stitching on one, and a baseball team print on the reverse. The same idea applies to a football shape as well, just space the varied-width and texture ribbon loops evenly around the perimeter.

SUPPLIES

Taggles Lovey pattern (page 144)

⅝ yard, solid-white fleece fabric (Front)

⅝ yard, team-print fleece fabric (Back)

1 yard, ⅜" red grosgrain ribbon (Baseball "stitches")

½ yard each, 4–5 different patterned and textured ribbons—You will need a total of 16, 4 inch lengths for the loops

Red all-purpose sewing thread (baseball stitching)

All-purpose thread

CUT

Using the pattern for Taggles Lovey, cut 1 from each the solid white fleece and the team-print fleece.

Cut red grosgrain ribbon into 10, 4 inch pieces.

Cut ribbons for loops into 16, 4 inch lengths.

SEW

1. To make the baseball stitching lines onto the white fleece circle, use a narrow 1.0 width and 2.0 length zigzag stitch to outline, taking care not to stretch fleece.

2. Place red ribbon strips, each folded into a "V" along the stitched line, spacing the ribbons evenly: 5 Vs on each stitched line. Stitch securely, close to the small fold on each ribbon piece.

3. Mark ribbon spacing along the raw edge of the embellished white fleece front. Fold each of the 16 ribbon loop pieces in half, wrong sides together. Baste close to the ends to hold. Place the ribbon loops along the edge, raw edges matching ribbon placement marks. Mix up the ribbons so that no two alike are placed beside one another. Baste ribbons through all layers to hold.

4. Place back, right sides together on embellished front, raw edges matching. Stitch seam, leaving a 3" opening for turning. Turn Lovey right side out.

5. Slip stitch opening closed. Finger press edges to neaten. Topstitch ½" from finished edge.

PLAYER ONESIE

Baby it's cold outside . . . but our little pumpkin needs to stay warm! Since mittens just fly off and get lost anyway, we added sleeves that flip over the hands to this cutie pie of a onesie. Fleece surgery logos and coordinating ribbon add sweet trims. Everyone will be gushing oohhs and aahhs over your little fan.

SUPPLIES

Long-sleeve onesie/bodysuit

⅜ yard, solid-color fleece

Scrap of fleece for team motif

½ yard, 1" printed grosgrain ribbon

All-purpose sewing thread

CUT

Trim sleeves from bodysuit; measure 4" down from shoulder, across width of each sleeve, and cut off lower sleeve. Use one as your pattern for the fleece sleeves.

Open seam of one sleeve. Lay opened sleeve on fleece lengthwise. Trace around sleeve, adding ½" seam allowances and extending sleeve 4" at the wrist end of sleeve. Cut 2 sleeves from fleece.

Trim motif from fleece ½" from team logo.

SEW:

1. Place fleece motif on front of bodysuit, 3" down from neckline, centered on bodysuit. Stitch ¼" away from edge, trim as needed.

2. On bodysuit, open each underarm seam 2" to allow room for reattaching fleece sleeves.

3. Finish the end of each sleeve with the finish desired (we serged ours but fold-over elastic would be a good choice, too) or leave unfinished.

4. On each sleeve, fold up 2" cuff to the right side of each sleeve. Fold sleeve in half lengthwise and mark center point on cuff. Stitch a perpendicular line through the cuff and sleeve layers along this center point to make two pockets. This holds the fold when you flip over the mitt at the end of the sleeves.

5. Right sides together, match fleece sleeves to bodysuit sleeve openings. Stitch seams. Finger press open.

6. Center ribbon trim over sleeve seams. Stitch on each long edge of ribbon trim to secure, taking care not to stretch the seams.

7. With the folded sleeve hems in place, match underarm seams, right sides together. Stitch seam, taking care that the hems match precisely.

8. Baby can wear sleeves as cuffs or you can flip over one side of cuff to form mitts to cover tiny hands, just like a mitten.

PLAYER LOUNGERS

Just like the lounge pants we created for the rest of the family, the littlest fan gets a cute pair too. Match these to the Player Onesie and the applause for your little player continues.

SUPPLIES

Commercial pajama pants pattern (to make into a one-piece pattern)

Pattern paper

Solid-color fleece, yardage to fit prepared pattern piece

Scrap of team-print fleece fabric (motif)

1 yard, 1" printed grosgrain ribbon (pant leg trim)

1⅓ yards, ⅜" grosgrain ribbon (ties at waist and pant leg trim)

⅝ yard, ⅜" braided elastic

All-purpose sewing thread

Steps for cutting are the same as Ladies Lazy-Day Capris (pages 64–65).

Trim team motif from team-print fleece fabric, leaving ½" excess around logo.

SEW

1. Right sides together, pin the front seam. Stitch seam 1", leave a 1" unstitched space (to create opening for ties), then continue stitching the remaining seam. Be sure to lockstitch or backstitch to secure stitches.

2. Finger press seam open. Stitch the opened seam allowance close to the seam line on both sides of the seam. Start at the upper waist edge, stitch down 2", securing the opened seam allowances to the pants. This will keep the seam allowance from folding over when the elastic is inserted. ·

3. Right sides together, pin the back seam. Stitch seam.

4. Stitch the trimmed motif to the back of the pants, right side approximately 2½" down from upper waist edge, centering motif right side up over the seam. Stitch ¼" away from motif edge, creating the fleece applique. Trim close to stitching as necessary.

5. Place ribbon trim on the lower portion of each leg. Measure 1½" from lower edge of each pant leg. Mark placement for trim. Place two ribbon trim pieces side by side, along the trim markings, stitch close to each long ribbon edge to secure.

6. Pin the inside leg seams, front to back, right sides together and stitch seam. Re-stitch this seam for extra strength.

7. Fold over 1" on the waist edge. Stitch close to the raw edge, forming the casing.

8. Turn under 1" hem on each pant leg. Stitch close to the raw edge on each hem.

9. Measure waist. Cut elastic for waist less 4". Stitch ribbon ties to each end of the elastic. Using a safety pin, insert elastic into the waist through the casing opening. Adjust elastic fullness and tie ribbon ends into a bow.

BOTTOMS-UP DIAPER COVER

We love fleece for its soft and fuzzy texture, but the added bonus of it being water resistant makes this fabric the perfect choice for a diaper cover. With this easy design you can make several adorable pairs.

SUPPLIES

Diaper Cover pattern (page 148)

⅜ yard each, 2 coordinating team-print fleece

2 yards, ⅜" braided elastic

⅓ yard, ⅜" grosgrain ribbon

All-purpose sewing thread

CUT

Choose pattern size for diaper cover. Cut diaper cover front from one team-print fleece and the diaper cover back from coordinating team-print fleece.

Cut 2, 6" ribbon lengths for waist ties.

SEW

1. Right sides together, place the front and back pieces together. Pin the right side seam. Stitch ¾". Leave a ¾" unstitched space (to create opening for ties), then continue stitching the remaining seam.

2. Finger press seam open. Stitch the opened seam close to seam line for 1½", securing the opened seam allowances to the garment. This will keep the seam allowance from folding over when the elastic is inserted.

3. Right sides together, stitch the left side seam and crotch seam. Turn under ¾" casing to wrong side of the waist and leg openings. Stitch close to raw edge of all the casings, leaving a 2" opening on each leg opening for inserting elastic.

4. Cut elastic pieces to size. Stitch ribbon ties to each end of the waistline elastic piece. Use a safety pin to thread elastic through the casing opening. Adjust and tie ribbon ends into a bow.

5. Using a safety pin, insert leg elastic pieces into casings. Adjust fit as desired. Overlap elastic ends, stitch to secure. Stitch the openings closed.

Seven

Man's Best Friend

WHO LEADS?

Customize a plain ready-made leash with this slipcover and clip-on mini bag holder. The "you-know-what" bags are easily pulled from the opening at the bottom, and can hold 2–3 plastic grocery bags or a roll of the mini bags you can pick up at the pet store. Walking the dog just got a Game Day style boost!

SUPPLIES

⅛ yard, solid-color fleece (Leash Cover)

¼ yard, coordinating solid-color fleece (Baggies Holder)

Purchased leash (web kind with hook on the end and loop handle)

6 inch, ¼" braided elastic

¼ yard, ⅜" grosgrain ribbon

1" D-ring

Fabric glue

All-purpose sewing thread

CUT

Measure the width and the length of leash (minus clip at end and handle loop).

Determine width of strip to be cut: Width of leash × 2, plus 1" for seam allowances.

Cut fleece strip for leash cover 60" long × width as calculated above.

Cut coordinating solid fleece into 8" × 10" rectangle.

Leash Cover

1. Right sides together, match raw edges of long side of fleece strip. Stitch seam. Turn tube right side out.
2. Trim tube to the length of leash. Set aside excess.
3. Use a large safety pin to thread leash through fleece tube. Position the tube over the leash webbing with seam positioned along one edge of the leash webbing.
4. Choose a wide decorative stitch on your sewing machine. Stitch through the center of tube, through all layers, the length of the tube, securing fleece cover to leash.
5. With remaining fleece tube piece, position seam along one side. Use the same decorative stitch as in step 4 to stitch through the center of tube as above. Cut into 2, 6" pieces. Tie one at lower end of leash cover in a loose overhand knot. Place a few drops of glue inside the knot then pull knot tight. Slip the D-ring on the remaining embellished strip. Loosely tie at upper end of leash cover, positioning D-ring so that it is on the underside of the leash. Place glue inside the knot, then pull knot tight. Let dry.

Bag Holder

1. Fold fleece rectangle, right sides together, matching 8" sides. Stitch seam.
2. Turn under 1" at upper and lower edges. Stitch close to raw edges at hem forming casings. Leave a 1" opening in casing seam on one end of holder for inserting elastic. On opposite end stitch casing all the way around.
3. On the end where casing is fully stitched, cut a small ¼" slit on right side of casing for ribbon. Use safety pin to thread ribbon thru this casing. Tie ribbon ends together.
4. On opposite end of holder, using a safety pin, thread elastic through casing. Tie elastic ends together so that there is a hole for baggies to be pulled out of holder. Tuck elastic ends to inside casing and holder.
5. Loop ribbon end of holder through D-ring on covered leash. Fill bag holder with recycled plastic sacks or baggies through drawstring opening at top of holder, pulling bags out through the elastic opening at bottom of holder as needed.

QUICK-STITCH PET BED

Keep your furry friends off the couch and resting in their own spot. Super easy to stitch up, this project is easy even for a newbie sewer to make in a flash. The square pillow insert is a simple slipcover (use this technique for a quickie throw pillow cover, too!), easy to remove and wash as needed. A plush, stuffed tube shaped around the pillow forms the square bed.

SUPPLIES

1 yard, fleece fabric for the bed ring

⅝ yard, fleece fabric for the pillow

All-purpose sewing thread

1 large bag polyester fiberfill

¼ yard, ¾" hook-and-loop tape

18" square pillow or pillow form

Cut 2, 18" × 45" pieces from fleece for tube.

Cut 1, 19" × 50" piece from fleece for pillow.

SEW

Bed Ring

1. Right sides together, stitch long edges, leaving an opening in the center, about 8" long, for stuffing. Turn tube right side out.
2. Stitch each end closed close to finished edge. Cut hook-and-loop tape to 8" long, rounding ends. Place the hook side strip to one end of tube on the outside edge, and the loop side strip to the opposite end on the inside edge (these will overlap and fasten together to form a ring). Stitch around all edges of each strip to secure.
3. Stuff the tube with polyester fiberfill. Slip stitch the opening closed to complete the bed. Fasten the ends closed to create the bed.

Pillow

1. Turn under 1" on each short end of fleece, forming a hem. Zigzag stitch over each hem edge to secure.
2. Lap fabric piece over pillow form with wrong side facing out. Pin overlap in place. Slip out pillow form.
3. Pin the side seams and stitch, taking care to not shift the hemmed edges.
4. Turn pillow cover right side out. Slip pillow inside.
5. Place the finished pillow into the center of the bed ring. Form the ring into a square shape by scooting the polyester fiberfill, to get the tube to form corners. Now, let sleeping dogs lie (in style).

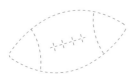

BRAIDED DOG TOY

Don't throw away those leftover fleece scraps! Fido is begging for a toy, and a braided bone created from strips of fleece will yield hours of tug o' war fun with your buddy. We braided this one with a handle, so you have a chance at actually winning the game they love to play.

SUPPLIES
⅛ yard each, 3 coordinating team-print or solid-color fleece

CUT
Cut 3, 4" × 48" strips, one of each fleece.

BRAID
1. Pull and stretch tight on each long strip to get fleece to curl inwards.
2. Hold strips together. Start braiding 20" from one end. Tip: Baste through the strips at the 20" point to hold strips together to make it easier to start the braid. If you have a small clamp or vise, use it to secure the strips to act as a "third hand" while you braid.
3. Braid tightly for 6", pulling on strips as you braid so that strips stay curled.
4. Bring loose unbraided ends together, and pair strips together so that you have 3 sets of strips. Braid the remaining toy to within 4" of end.
5. To finish, take 2 strips closest to outside of braid, loop them around braid, then slip both ends through to form knot. Pull very tight and trim ends.

MOUSEY CAT TOY

Kitties LOVE to bat things about, and a "mouse" toy is a bunch of fun for the both of you. Relieve some stress (yours and theirs)—fill this toy with some catnip and watch them go flying for the fleece critter. Taking a break from your hectic day to play with your best friend . . . priceless!

SUPPLIES

¼ yard, solid-color fleece fabric
¼ yard, ⅜" satin ribbon (tail)
¼ yard, ⅜" grosgrain ribbon (bow)
1 jingle bell
Polyester fiberfill
All-purpose sewing thread
Catnip (optional)

CUT

Cut 1, 5" × 9" rectangle from fleece.

SEW

1. Right sides together, matching 5" sides, fold fabric piece. Stitch this side and lower edge seam.
2. Fold ribbon in half, matching ends. Finger press seam open on open end of toy. Match remaining raw edges and make into a 3D triangle shape by centering opened seam on opposite end. Tuck ribbon inside piece with folded edge to be caught in the seam on one of the corners. Stitch seam, leaving a 2" opening in center to turn and stuff.
3. Turn toy right side out. Add small amount of stuffing, insert jingle bell, and add catnip if desired. Stuff remainder of toy lightly. Slip stitch opening closed.
4. Position "mouse" so that the ribbon ends are the tail, on the base of the toy. Hand tack bow trim in place, 1½" down from top "nose" of Mousey Cat Toy.

DOGGIE HOODIE

Dress up the pup in a warm hoodie designed especially for your little angel. Our little furry fan makes its own fashion statement with a coat sporting fleece bones as trim for a little extra pizazz. Cut the little bone shapes from contrast colors of fleece, with no edge finishing required.

SUPPLIES

Doggie Hoodie pattern (page 149)
½ yard, solid-color fleece (Hoodie)
⅛ yard, 2 contrasting solid-color fleece
   (Dog Bone Trim)
All-purpose sewing thread

CUT

Using the Doggie Hoodie body and
   hood patterns, cut 1 body and
   2 hoods.
Cut 2, 4" squares from scraps for leg
   hole facings.
Using the bone pattern, cut 5 from
   each fleece for a total of 10
   bones.

SEW

1. Using hoodie pattern, mark leg holes. Center square leg hole facing piece on right side of each leg hole. Stitch following markings. Trim away opening to ¼" of leg hole stitching, clip and turn facing to the wrong side of hoodie. Topstitch ½" away from leg hole finished edge. Trim facing around leg hole close to topstitching.

2. Starting ¾" from raw edge of hoodie, and using alternating colors along hoodie edge, lay 9 dog bone cut-outs end to end. Stitch through the center of each bone to secure to hoodie.

3. Right sides together, match hood pieces. Stitch hood seam. Turn under ½" hem along hood opening (not neck edge). Stitch to secure.

4. Right sides together, place hood to neck edge, matching hood seam to center back of neckline. Stitch seam.

5. Right sides together, match front seam on dog hoodie. Stitch. Finger press the neckline seam of the hood towards the dog hoodie. Topstitch seam allowance at front neck opening. Stitch remaining bone cut-out at neck opening through center of bone to create the bow tie.

Eight

Low-Sew and No-Sew Throws and Pillows

TIE-DOWN PILLOW

No sewing required to make this clipped-and-tied pillow. Let all your friends get in on the act, too. Just be sure to grab a sharp pair of shears to cut the fringe strips. Even kids can learn to tie the basic overhand knot—the trick to keep the fringe lying flat and smooth. These make perfect toss-around floor pillows, and are an easy change-out cover for tired pillows.

SUPPLIES

⅞ yard, team-print fleece

⅞ yard, solid-color fleece

Acrylic fringe-cut ruler

Rotary cutter and mat

Pillow insert (here 18" × 18")

CUT AND TIE

1. Trim both fabric pieces to measure 28" × 28". Wrong sides together, matching raw edges, layer each of the fleece pieces.
2. Mark 5" in from raw edges on all sides, creating a line as a guide for fringe.
3. Following the 5" markings that overlap at the corners, trim away corners through both fleece layers. With an acrylic fringe-ruler as a guide, cut 1" wide fringe strips up to the 5" mark through both fleece layers using rotary cutter. Continue cutting fringe on one side of pillow until entire edge is fringed. If you do not have an acrylic fringe-cut ruler and rotary cutter, you can use a sharp pair of shears and a 1" wide ruler to make the fringe cuts.
4. With both layers together, tie each of the fringe strips into an overhand knot. Continue knotting fringe, taking care to keep knots in alignment and even along the pillow edge. Complete the fringe knots on one edge, then rotate pillow layers and repeat from step three until three sides are complete.
5. Trim fringe for remaining pillow edge. Slip pillow insert inside cover. Continue to knot fringe until pillow is complete.

Note: Tie-Down Pillows can be made in just about any size you desire. Measure your pillow insert and add 10" to each side to determine the size to cut the fleece before fringing. Finished size of the pillow will be 10" less in width and length, after trimming and tying the fringe.

TIE-DOWN THROW

The original fleece throw, this one is tied in the same overhand knotted fringe as the Tie-Down Pillow. Choose to make yours in a single layer or double up for twice the warmth and color.

SUPPLIES

  2 yards, team-print fleece
  2 yards, solid-color fleece
  Acrylic fringe-cut ruler
  Rotary cutter and mat

CUT AND TIE

1. Trim selvages and edges on both fabric pieces to measure 58" × 70". Wrong sides together, matching raw edges, layer each of the fleece pieces.
2. Follow steps 2–4 as for Tie-Down Pillow, until all four sides of throw are complete. Trim fringe for remaining edge. Continue to knot fringe until throw is complete.

Note: Tie-Down blankets and throws can be made in just about any size you desire, taking into consideration the 60" width of the fleece. Finished size of the blanket or throw will be 10" less in width and length, after trimming and tying the fringe.

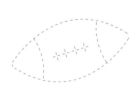

CLIP-AND-FLIP LAP BLANKET

This twist on fringe is made with a clip-and-flip-through technique that gives a nice contrast border on the top side. Make this any size you choose, just allow enough room around the outside edges to clip the fringe strips.

SUPPLIES

1¼ yards, team-print fleece
1¼ yards, solid-color fleece
Acrylic fringe-cut ruler
Rotary cutter and mat
Craft knife or blade-type buttonhole cutter

CUT AND FLIP

1. Trim selvages and edges on both fabric pieces, to measure 44" × 44". Wrong sides together, matching raw edges, layer each of the fleece pieces.
2. Mark 4" in from raw edges on all sides, creating a line as a guide for fringe.
3. Following the 4" markings that overlap at the corners, trim away corners through both fleece layers. With an acrylic fringe-cut ruler as a guide, cut 1"-wide fringe strips up to the 4" mark through both fleece layers with rotary cutter. Continue cutting fringe on one side of blanket until entire edge is fringed. If you do not have an acrylic fringe-cut ruler and rotary cutter, you can use a sharp pair of shears and 1" wide ruler to make the fringe cuts.
4. With a craft knife or buttonhole cutter, make a ½" slit through both fleece layers, directly below the 4" guide line, centering slit in width of each fringe piece. Trim ends of each of the fringe layers at a 45-degree angle.
5. With each fringe layered set, push both fringe pieces through slit towards underside of blanket. Pull on ends of fringe set to snap fringe into place in slit, forming a knot. Repeat until the entire side of blanket is complete.
6. Rotate blanket and repeat from step 3 until all sides are complete.

Note: The finished size of the blanket will be 8" less in width and length, after clipping and flipping the fringe.

PATTERNS AND TEMPLATES

Basic Beanie (Baby, Child, Adult)

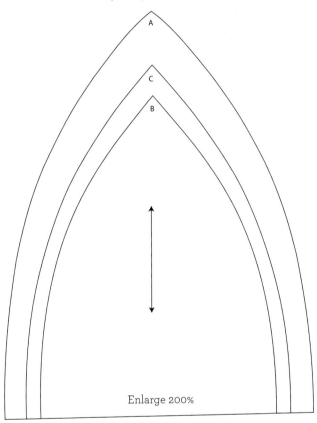

A

C

B

Enlarge 200%

Fingerless Arm Warmers

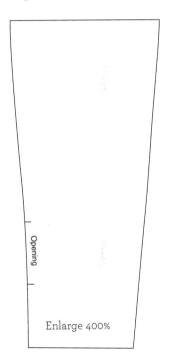

Opening

Enlarge 400%

Ear Warmer Headband

Hot Hands Mitts

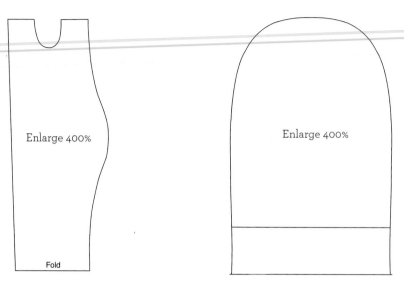

Enlarge 400%

Fold

Enlarge 400%

Taggles Lovey

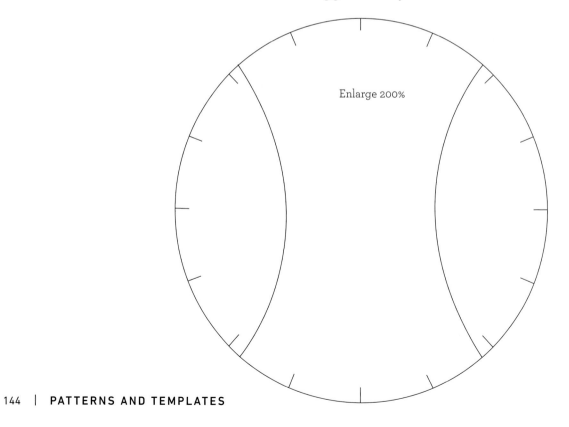

Enlarge 200%

Lace-Up Coffee Cozy

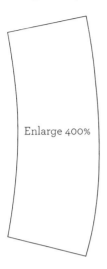

Enlarge 400%

Flower Power Headwrap

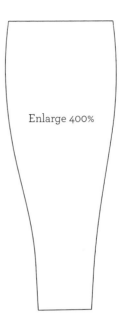

Enlarge 400%

Rain Delay Boot Liners

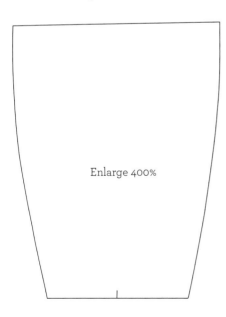

Enlarge 400%

Show-Me Shrug

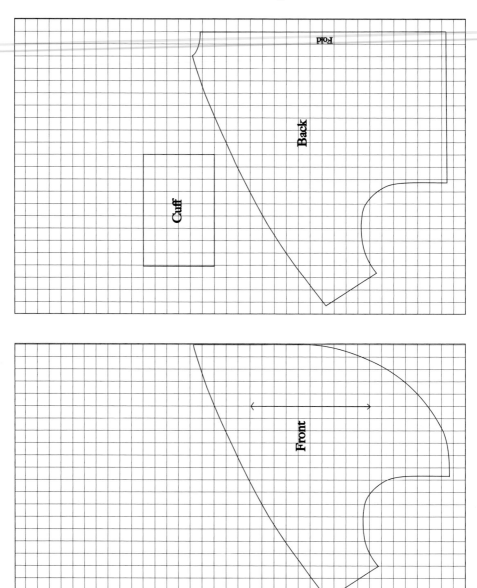

1 sq=1 inch

Braids Beanie

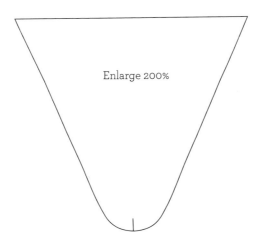

Enlarge 200%

Earflaps Beanie

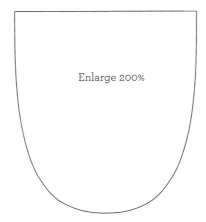

Enlarge 200%

Reversible Pullover Bib

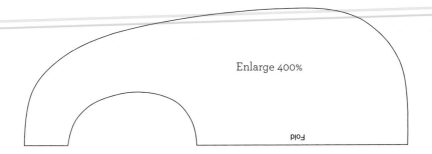

Enlarge 400%

Fold

Bottoms-Up Diaper Cover

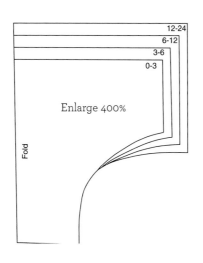

12-24

6-12

3-6

0-3

Enlarge 400%

Fold

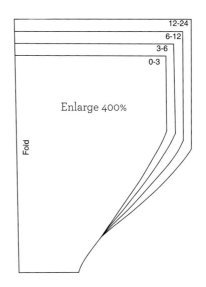

12-24

6-12

3-6

0-3

Enlarge 400%

Fold

Doggie Hoodie

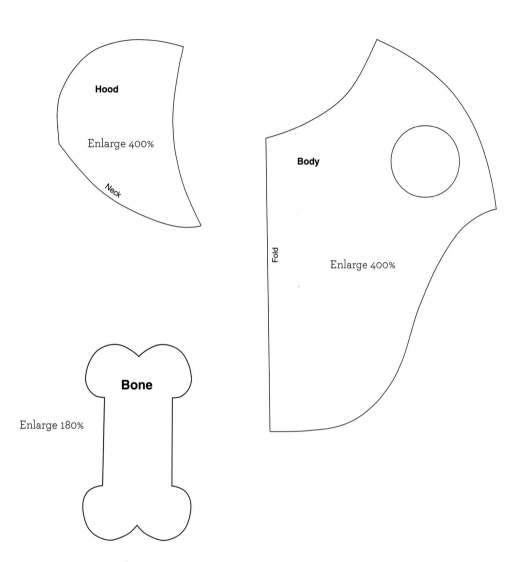

Hood

Enlarge 400%

Neck

Body

Fold

Enlarge 400%

Bone

Enlarge 180%

TEAM COLOR CHARTS

Find all your favorite teams here and their official colors!

NFL TEAM COLORS

ARIZONA CARDINALS	Cardinal Red, Black, White
ATLANTA FALCONS	Red, Black, White, Silver
BALTIMORE RAVENS	Black, Purple, Metallic Gold, White
BUFFALO BILLS	Royal Blue, Red, White, Navy
CAROLINA PANTHERS	Black, Panther Blue, Silver, White
CHICAGO BEARS	Dark Navy, Orange, White
CINCINNATI BENGALS	Black, Brilliant Orange, White
CLEVELAND BROWNS	Brown, Orange, White
DALLAS COWBOYS	Navy, Silver, White
DENVER BRONCOS	Broncos Navy, Orange, White
DETROIT LIONS	Honolulu Blue, Silver, Black, White
GREEN BAY PACKERS	Dark Green, Gold, White
HOUSTON TEXANS	Deep Steel Blue, Battle Red, Liberty White
INDIANAPOLIS COLTS	Royal Blue, White
JACKSONVILLE JAGUARS	Teal, Black, White, Gold
KANSAS CITY CHIEFS	Red, Gold, White
MIAMI DOLPHINS	Aqua, Coral, Navy, White
MINNESOTA VIKINGS	Purple, Gold, White
NEW ENGLAND PATRIOTS	Nautical Blue, Red, New Century Silver, White
NEW ORLEANS SAINTS	Old Gold, Black, White
NEW YORK GIANTS	Dark Blue, Red, Gray, White
NEW YORK JETS	Hunter Green, White
OAKLAND RAIDERS	Silver, Black, White
PHILADELPHIA EAGLES	Midnight Green, Black, Charcoal, Silver, White
PITTSBURGH STEELERS	Black, Gold, White
ST. LOUIS RAMS	Millennium Blue, New Century Gold, White
SAN DIEGO CHARGERS	Navy, Gold, Powder Blue, White
SAN FRANCISCO 49ERS	49ers Red, Metallic Gold, White
SEATTLE SEAHAWKS	College Navy, Wolf Grey, Action Green, White
TAMPA BAY BUCCANEERS	Buccaneer Red, Pewter, Black, Orange, White
TENNESSEE TITANS	Navy, Titans Blue, White
WASHINGTON REDSKINS	Burgundy, Gold, White

MLB TEAM COLORS

ARIZONA DIAMONDBACKS	Sedona Red, Black, Sonoran Sand, White
ATLANTA BRAVES	Navy, Scarlet, White
BALTIMORE ORIOLES	Orange, Black, White
BOSTON RED SOX	Midnight Navy, Red, White
CHICAGO CUBS	Blue, Red, White
CHICAGO WHITE SOX	Black, Silver, White
CINCINNATI REDS	Red, Black, White
CLEVELAND INDIANS	Navy, Red, White
COLORADO ROCKIES	Black, Purple, Silver, White
DETROIT TIGERS	Midnight Navy, White, Orange
HOUSTON ASTROS	Navy, Orange, Light Orange, Gray, White
KANSAS CITY ROYALS	Royal Blue, White
LOS ANGELES ANGELS OF ANAHEIM	Red, Dark Red, Midnight Navy, Silver, White
LOS ANGELES DODGERS	Dodger Blue, White, Red
MIAMI MARLINS	Black, Red-Orange, Silver, White, Blue, Yellow
MILWAUKEE BREWERS	Navy, Metallic Gold, White
MINNESOTA TWINS	Navy, Scarlet Red, White
NEW YORK METS	Mets Blue, Orange, White
NEW YORK YANKEES	Midnight Navy, White
OAKLAND ATHLETICS	Green, Gold, White
PHILADELPHIA PHILLIES	Red, White, Blue
PITTSBURGH PIRATES	Black, Gold, White
ST. LOUIS CARDINALS	Red, Midnight Navy, White
SAN DIEGO PADRES	Navy, White, Sand
SAN FRANCISCO GIANTS	Black, Orange, White
SEATTLE MARINERS	Navy, Northwest Green, Metallic Silver, White
TAMPA BAY RAYS	Navy, Columbia Blue, White, Gold
TEXAS RANGERS	Blue, Red, White
TORONTO BLUE JAYS	Royal Blue, White, Navy, Red
WASHINGTON NATIONALS	Red, Blue, White

NBA TEAM COLORS

ATLANTA HAWKS	Navy, Red, Silver, White
BOSTON CELTICS	Celtic Green, White
BROOKLYN NETS	Black, White
CHARLOTTE BOBCATS	Navy, Light Blue, Orange, Cool Gray, White

CHICAGO BULLS	Red, Black, White
CLEVELAND CAVALIERS	Wine, Gold, White
DALLAS MAVERICKS	Navy, Light Royal, Silver, White
DENVER NUGGETS	Light Blue, Navy, Yellow Gold, White
DETROIT PISTONS	Royal Blue, Red, White
GOLDEN STATE WARRIORS	Royal Blue, California Golden Yellow, White
HOUSTON ROCKETS	Red, White, Black, Silver
INDIANA PACERS	Navy, Gold, Gray, White
LOS ANGELES CLIPPERS	Red, Royal Blue, White
LOS ANGELES LAKERS	Royal Purple, Gold, White
MEMPHIS GRIZZLIES	Memphis Midnight Blue, Beale Street Blue, Smoke Blue, Grizzlies Gold, White
MIAMI HEAT	Black, Deep Red, White, Yellow
MILWAUKEE BUCKS	Hunter Green, Dark Red, Silver, White
MINNESOTA TIMBERWOLVES	Slate Blue, Black, Silver, White
NEW ORLEANS PELICANS	Creole Blue, Dark Purple, Mardi Gras Gold, White
NEW YORK KNICKERBOCKERS (THE KNICKS)	Blue, Orange, Silver, White
OKLAHOMA CITY THUNDER	Strong Blue, Navy, Red-Orange, Yellow, White
ORLANDO MAGIC	Light Royal, Black, Silver, White
PHILADELPHIA 76ERS	Red, Royal Blue, White
PHOENIX SUNS	Purple, Burnt Orange, Gray, White
PORTLAND TRAIL BLAZERS	Black, Red, Silver, White
SACRAMENTO KINGS	Purple, Black, Silver, White
SAN ANTONIO SPURS	Black, Silver, White
TORONTO RAPTORS	Red, Black, Silver, White
UTAH JAZZ	Navy, Dark Green, Dark Yellow, White
WASHINGTON WIZARDS	Red, Navy, Silver, White

NHL TEAM COLORS

ANAHEIM DUCKS	Black, Gold, Orange, White
BOSTON BRUINS	Black, Gold, White
BUFFALO SABRES	Navy, Gold, Aluminum Silver, White
CALGARY FLAMES	Red, Gold, Black, White
CAROLINA HURRICANES	Red, Black, Silver, White
CHICAGO BLACKHAWKS	Red, Black, White
COLORADO AVALANCHE	Burgundy, Steel Blue, Black, Silver, White
COLUMBUS BLUE JACKETS	Union Blue, Goal Red, Capital Silver, White

DALLAS STARS	Black, Green, Gold, White
DETROIT RED WINGS	Red, White
EDMONTON OILERS	Royal Blue, Orange, White
FLORIDA PANTHERS	Red, Navy, Gold, Yellow, White
LOS ANGELES KINGS	Black, Aluminum Silver, White
MINNESOTA WILD	Forest Green, Iron Range Red, Harvest Gold, Minnesota Wheat, White
MONTREAL CANADIENS	Red, Blue, White
NASHVILLE PREDATORS	Gold, Dark Blue, White
NEW JERSEY DEVILS	Red, Black, White
NEW YORK ISLANDERS	Royal Blue, Orange, White
NEW YORK RANGERS	Blue, Red, White
OTTAWA SENATORS	Red, Black, Gold, White
PHILADELPHIA FLYERS	Orange, Black, White
PHOENIX COYOTES	Brick Red, White, Black, Desert Sand
PITTSBURGH PENGUINS	Black, Vegas Gold, White
ST. LOUIS BLUES	Blue, Gold, Dark Blue, White
SAN JOSE SHARKS	Deep Pacific Teal, Black, Burnt Orange, White
TAMPA BAY LIGHTNING	Blue, White
TORONTO MAPLE LEAFS	Blue, White
VANCOUVER CANUCKS	Blue, Green, Silver, White
WASHINGTON CAPITALS	Red, Navy, White
WINNIPEG JETS	Polar Night Blue, Aviator Blue, Silver, White

NCAA TEAM COLORS

ALABAMA CRIMSON TIDE	Crimson, Black, Gray, White
APPALACHIAN STATE MOUNTAINEERS	Black, Gold
ARIZONA WILDCATS	Cardinal, Navy
ARIZONA STATE SUN DEVILS	Sun Devil Maroon, Gold
ARKANSAS RAZORBACKS	Cardinal, White
AUBURN TIGERS	Burnt Orange, Navy
BOISE STATE BRONCOS	Blue, Orange
BRIGHAM YOUNG COUGARS	Blue, White
CALIFORNIA GOLDEN BEARS	Blue, Gold
CINCINNATI BEARCATS	Red, Black, Tan, White
CLEMSON TIGERS	Orange, Purple, White
COLORADO BUFFALOES	Black, Gold

DUKE BLUE DEVILS	Royal Blue, White
EAST CAROLINA PIRATES	Purple, Gold
FLORIDA GATORS	Green, Orange, Blue, Black, White
FLORIDA STATE SEMINOLES	Garnet, Gold
GEORGIA BULLDOGS	Red, Black
GEORGIA TECH YELLOW JACKETS	Old Gold, White, Navy
IDAHO VANDALS	Silver, Gold, Black, White
ILLINOIS FIGHTING ILLINI	Orange, Blue
IOWA HAWKEYES	Gold, Black
IOWA STATE CYCLONES	Cardinal, Gold
KANSAS JAYHAWKS	Red, Blue, Yellow, White
KANSAS STATE WILDCATS	Purple, White
KENTUCKY WILDCATS	Blue, White
LOUISIANA TECH BULLDOGS	Blue, Red
LOUISVILLE CARDINALS	Red, Black
LSU TIGERS	Purple, Gold
MARYLAND TERRAPINS	Red, White, Black, Gold
MIAMI HURRICANES	Orange, Green, White
MICHIGAN WOLVERINES	Maize, Blue
MICHIGAN STATE SPARTANS	Green, White
MINNESOTA GOLDEN GOPHERS	Maroon, Gold
MISSISSIPPI REBELS	Cardinal, Navy
MISSISSIPPI STATE BULLDOGS	Maroon, White
MISSOURI TIGERS	Black, Old Gold
MONTANA GRIZZLIES	Maroon, Silver
NEBRASKA CORNHUSKERS	Scarlet, Cream
NORTH CAROLINA TAR HEELS	Carolina Blue, White
NORTH CAROLINA STATE WOLFPACK	Red, White
OKLAHOMA SOONERS	Crimson, Cream, Gray, White
OKLAHOMA STATE COWBOYS	Orange, Black, White
OREGON DUCKS	Thunder Green, Lightning Yellow
OREGON STATE BEAVERS	Orange, Black
PENN STATE NITTANY LIONS	Navy, White
PITTSBURGH PANTHERS	Blue, Gold, White
PURDUE BOILERMAKERS	Old Gold, Black
SOUTH CAROLINA GAMECOCKS	Garnet, Black, White
SOUTHERN ILLINOIS SALUKIS	Maroon, White
TENNESSEE VOLUNTEERS	Tennessee Orange, White

NCAA TEAM COLORS CONTINUED

TEXAS LONGHORNS	Burnt Orange, White
TEXAS A&M AGGIES	Maroon, White
TEXAS TECH RED RAIDERS	Red, Black, White
UCLA BRUINS	True Blue, Gold
USC TROJANS	Cardinal, Gold, White
UTAH UTES	Crimson, White
VANDERBILT UNIVERSITY	Black, Gold
VIRGINIA CAVALIERS	Blue, Orange, White
VIRGINIA TECH HOKIES	Maroon, Orange, White
WASHINGTON HUSKIES	Purple, Gold, White
WASHINGTON STATE COUGARS	Crimson, Gray, White
WEST VIRGINIA MOUNTAINEERS	Navy Blue, Old Gold, White
WESTERN MICHIGAN BRONCOS	Brown, Gold, White, Black
WISCONSIN BADGERS	Cardinal, White, Black

CORN HOLE GAME

Cornhole has become THE game for both tailgating and backyard fun. The rules of the game are pretty simple—one of the reasons folks love this sport. Try it and you will find it to be as addicting as we did! And if you get ambitious and want to make your own personalized boards, here are the instructions for you to hand off to your best woodworking friend (or dad, in my case).

EQUIPMENT

Two Corn Hole Boards

24" × 48" is regulation size, with 6" hole centered horizontally and 9" from top of board.

Back of each board is propped up 12" off of the ground.

8 Corn Hole Bags

6" × 6" is regulation size, 4 each of two different colors. Each bag is filled with 14 to 16 ounces of dried whole kernel corn. Bags are made of sturdy fabric, such as duck cloth (our inserts are made from this and refillable, then placed into the fleece team-colors covers).

HOW TO PLAY

* Place front of boards 27 feet apart, on level ground.
* Each player stands in his area next to the board—do not step over the "foul line" or the front of the board while tossing.
* Bags are tossed by each player on a side (or alternately by each player on a side if playing doubles), until all the players' bags are down range.
* When all 8 bags have been thrown by each side, the points are added up and this is one round of play. The team that scores the most points begins tossing the next round.

The goal is to get to 21!

* 3 points (Ringer)—Bag goes into hole by way of an awesome shot into the hole, slides on board and drops into hole, or is pushed into hole by another bag from either team.

* 1 point—Bag lands on the board and rests on the board. If a bag bounces on the ground and then onto the board no points are awarded.

* 0 points—Bag is resting half on ground and half on board. Any bag that lands on the ground, or is knocked off the board by another bag, no points are awarded.

* Cancellation of points—Corn Hole game totals are by way of point cancellation, NOT just total points scored! If a 3-point ringer is thrown by an opponent, that cancels out the other team's ringer. Same with a 1 pointer on the board, this cancels out an opponent's 1 pointer. Example: If Team A scores a total of 5 points, and Team B scores a total of 1 point, Team A has earned 4 points and Team B, the opponent 0.

Make Your Own Corn Hole Boards!

MATERIALS TO MAKE TWO CORN HOLE GAME BOARDS

2, 2' x 4' x ½" presanded plywood (for game board top)

4, 2" x 3" x 8' studs (for game board frame and legs)

Note: look for studs that are straight, not warped or twisted

4, $\frac{5}{16}$" x 3½" carriage bolts

4, $\frac{5}{16}$" fender washers

4, $\frac{5}{16}$" wing nuts

1¼" finishing nail (#16 or larger)

Wood glue

Wood filler

120-grit sand paper

Enamel paint primer

High-gloss enamel paint

Miter saw or circular saw

Jigsaw

Drill with ⁵⁄₁₆" and ½" drill bits

Nail set

Hammer

Measuring tape and pencil

Safety glasses

1. From the 2 × 3 studs cut four side pieces to fit the length of the plywood. Set remaining stud pieces aside for later.
2. Using the ⁵⁄₁₆" drill bit, drill holes through the center of each side piece, 2¾" in from one end. You will have two side pieces with holes for each board.
3. Apply the wood glue to one long 2" edge of a side piece. Place the side piece on one upside down piece of plywood, glue side down, aligning the piece with the outside edge of the longer side. Do the same with the other piece along the opposite edge, keeping the holes on same end.
4. When glue is dry, turn piece over and nail each side piece in place with finishing nails. Set nails ⅛" below surface of plywood. Repeat for the second piece of plywood.
5. Measure the space between the inside of the side pieces along the top and bottom edges and in the middle. From the remaining stud pieces, cut the front, back, and middle pieces to that length. From the leftover stud pieces cut four legs 11½" long. You will have three cross pieces and two legs for each board.
6. Using the ½" drill bit, drill holes through the center of each leg piece, 1¼" from end. Set legs aside.
7. Apply the wood glue to the one long 2" edge and to both 2" ends of the two front, two back, and two middle pieces. Place the pieces on the upside down pieces of plywood, glue side down, aligning the front and back pieces flush with outside edge of plywood, and placing the third piece midway from each end. When glue is dry, turn over and nail each piece in place with finishing nails. Set nails ⅛" below surface of plywood.

8. Draw a 6" circle on the top end (the same end with drilled holes in the side pieces) of the piece of plywood, centering the opening from the side edges of the plywood and 9" from the top edge.

9. Drill a ½" diameter hole through the plywood inside of the 6" circle for the jigsaw blade. Carefully cut out the holes with the jigsaw and sand edges smooth. Repeat for second piece of plywood.

10. To finish: Fill all nail holes with wood filler. Let dry at least 2 hours. Sand wood filler holes and all outside edges smooth. Coat the tops, sides, and underneath of the finished game board and the legs with a coat of primer and at least two coats of high-gloss enamel paint of your choice. Let dry completely.

11. To assemble: Push the carriage bolts through the holes on the side pieces of the finished game board from the outside and tap the bolts with hammer until heads are flush with the wood. Place the legs over the bolts and fasten to frame using the washers and wing nuts to hold in place. The legs can be stored inside of frame by loosening the wing nuts and rotating them 90° and retightening the nuts to hold them in place.

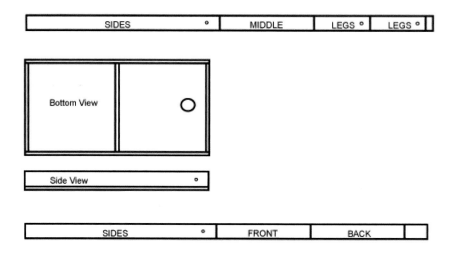

ACKNOWLEDGMENTS

The saying goes "it takes a village," and nothing is truer concerning the group of people necessary to make *Game Day* possible. So in the spirit of sincere gratitude, I would like to thank all of you who helped, pushed, prodded, encouraged, energized, and worked with me to bring this project to fruition. *Game Day* would not have arrived without you.

To Mom and Dad, you have always encouraged me to be the best form of myself I could be. Thank you for all the hours you both devoted to this book. Dad is my fact-checker, list-maker, and woodworker extraordinaire. Your Corn Hole Boards are perfect! We lost my mom this past year as I was writing and creating projects for this book. Mom, I miss your words of wisdom each and every day. Know that you passed on your love of family and the importance of putting family first.

To Allyce King, my daughter and business partner in crime, thanks for being my daily sounding board—formulating project design ideas and helping perfect the patterns for all of our projects. Through both laughter and tears we manage to continue on our path to bring new ideas to fruition for both DIYStyle and Allyce King Swim.

To Jonathan Cummins and his young family, thank you for your continued patience through this challenging year, and for knowing just the right time to pop in with my grandson, Jameson. You, Tori, and Jameson added several bright spots in my overscheduled days.

To my sisters, I would have never made it to here without the two of you! Peggy West helped with my first-pass edits and Linda Bean tied many blankets and kept me company. But the constant love and support you both gave during a really hard time is what really mattered. I thank both of you for all the PME (Positive Mental Energy), and for always being there when I need you most.

And to all of my many friends and relatives who were continually sending me kind words on Facebook to "keep going," I loved all of your messages! I look to Facebook to give me a dose of humor and an energy fix, and am seldom let down. Without Facebook I would have not been able to stay so close to all of your daily goings-on and still be able to be in my writing bubble.

Several people and companies gave products for me to work with for *Game Day*. Special thanks to Janome, Babylock, Prym-Dritz, A&E, VELCRO USA, June Tailor, and Clover-USA. And what would this book be without fabric?! Thanks to Sykel, Fabric Traditions, and David Textiles, for your generosity and guiding me in the proper use of these licensed fleece fabrics.

This book would not be complete without some beautiful photos, showcasing all of the projects and supplies in *Game Day*. A world of thanks goes to Jack Deutsch and his team (that included my editor, BJ Berti, styling!) in New York City, for the lovely project photos. And Carmen Troesser, it was a good day when I found you "around the corner"! Thank you for jumping in to do all of the notions and supplies photos on such short notice, to keep me on schedule.

And lastly, but certainly not least, a huge thank-you, to BJ Berti and Jasmine Faustino, and the entire crew at St. Martin's Press, for being behind this book project and sharing my vision for *Game Day*. It has been quite the winding road, but we made it to our destination!

And to anyone who I may have not thanked personally, please know your kind thoughts and words of encouragement were all needed and much appreciated. Yes, it takes a village, and I was so very fortunate to be the center of a very special one.

RESOURCES

FLEECE FABRIC PRODUCERS

Sykel, Collegiate NCAA-licensed team fleece fabrics   sykelenterprises.com

Fabric Traditions, NFL- and MLB-licensed team fleece fabrics
   fabrictraditions.com

David Textiles, Inc. Solid colors and sports-print fleece fabrics
   davidtextilesinc.com

ONLINE FABRIC RETAILERS

Jo-Ann Fabric and Craft Stores   joann.com

Hancock Fabrics   hancockfabrics.com

Fabric.com   fabric.com

Vogue Fabrics   voguefabricsstore.com

NOTIONS AND TOOLS

American & Efrid Mills, Inc.   amefird.com/consumer-products

Coats & Clark   coatsandclark.com

Schmetz Needles   schmetzneedles.com

Clover Needlecraft, Inc.   clover-usa.com

June Tailor   junetailor.com

OLFA Products   olfaproducts.com

Pellon Products   pellonideas.com

Mountain Mist   mountainmistlp.com

Aleene's   ilovetocreate.com

ELASTICS, TRIMS, AND FASTENERS

VELCRO® BRAND   velcro.com

Prym Consumer Products   prymconsumerusa.com

Berwick Offray, LLC   offray.com

MACHINES

Janome America, Inc.   janome.com

Baby Lock, USA   babylock.com

Bernina USA   bernina.com

DIYSTYLE INSPIRATION AND INSTRUCTION

diystyle.net

facebook.com/diystyle

pinterest.com/diystyle

youtube.com/diystylevodcasts

twitter.com#diystyle

INDEX